S0-BYR-087

ADVANCE PRAISE

"Our children are now living in an age where social media is central to their lives. You need to read this book to understand the dangers they face and what you need to do to keep them safe."

- Steve Young, NFL Hall of Famer and father of 4

"You may think that identity theft can't happen to your children, or if it does you may believe they are so young it's not a big deal. This book shows you it is a very big deal, and what you need to do about it."

- John Lauck, CEO of Children's Miracle Network Hospitals

"Joe Mason is an expert in how to prevent child identity theft, and how to recover from it should your child become a victim. If you are a parent you need to learn from him."

- Brian Hazelgren, philanthropist, best-selling author, father of 6

"Every parent, whether your child is six months, six years, or sixteen, needs to read this book."

- Amy Lupold Bair, ResorucefulMommy.com, mother of 2

"As a concerned father of two, I'm ready to join author Joe Mason and say "Enough is enough!" Parents need to stand up to perpetrators of identity theft -- buying, and reading, this book is one way to do just that."

- Jeff Rosenblum, Producer of The Naked Brand documentary, father of 2

"Wow. I did not realize what a problem child identity theft has become until I read this book. Now I know how the everyday things my kids and I do can make us vulnerable."

– John Schneider, Actor, CMNH Co-Founder and father of 3

"As a journalist, it's imperative that we warn parents about child identify theft. As a mother—reading "Bankrupt at Birth" armed me with crucial information to prevent my own child from becoming a victim."

-Audra Lowe, Host of "The Better Show" and mom

BANKRUPT AT BIRTH

WHY CHILD IDENTITY THEFT IS ON THE RISE & HOW IT'S HAPPENING UNDER PARENTS' NOSES

Joe Mason

with Steve Schwartz

Printed in the U.S.A. by Signature Book Printing, www.sbpbooks.com

Published in the United States by Nimble Cricket Press

ISBN: 978-1-936984-11-4

Library of Congress Control Number: 2012945850

Edited by Darla Bruno

Cover and Interior Design by Ann Alger, Karen Burton and Doreen Hann

All Photos of Joe Mason and his family courtesy of KhadijaPervez.com

BANKRUPT AT BIRTH

WHY CHILD IDENTITY THEFT IS ON THE RISE & HOW IT'S HAPPENING UNDER PARENTS' NOSES

BANKRUPT AT BIRTH

ADDITIONAL RESOURCES

To accompany the book, we've included invaluable bonus materials so you can proactively protect your children against identity theft.

Throughout the book, you'll see Shield Icons that will point you where to go to collect your free resources. Here's what you'll get:

- » The Quick Start Guide to Child ID Theft
- » The Daily Shield Identity Theft eBook
- » Risk Factors Checklist
- » The Child ID Theft Safety Tele-class
- » Video: Child ID Theft: A Growing Problem
- » 10 Ways to Protect Your Smartphone, Laptop and Tablet
- » Video: Emily's Story
- » 30-Day trial of IDENTITY GUARD®†

Visit **www.BankruptAtBirthBook.com**
for additional resources.

DEDICATION

To Emily & Chase.

At its heart, this book was written for you.

You are my greatest gifts.

ACKNOWLEDGEMENTS

When I decided it was time to spread the word about child identity theft with a book, I knew it was going to be a team effort. Educating people about how to protect themselves from identity theft is something we do for a living, but the audience for this book, specifically parents, would require a different type of message – a message that would have to resonate with busy, time-starved, and often sleep-deprived parents. So, had it not been for the support of our family, friends, and colleagues, there is no chance that this book – and the powerful message within – would resonate with parents, much less ever go to print. We certainly couldn't have done this without them, and we'd like to give our heartfelt gratitude and specifically acknowledge:

» Angela Lauria – for being an outstanding advisor, coach, and for overseeing the project from inception to publication.

» Bob Wagman – for his mastery in helping to bring these ideas to life, for his tenacity, and for providing extraordinary research and creativity.

Additionally, there are hundreds of colleagues at Intersections who build and maintain the systems and technology that help protect the identities of millions of adults and children across this country. Many of these same people shared their knowledge, insights, and technical expertise for this book, and we'd like to especially recognize:

» Michael Stanfield – for believing in us, encouraging us, and giving us the opportunity to make a difference.

» Wendy Weinberger – for being a great thought partner, legal advisor, and passionate advocate of protecting kids.

» The people and teams at Intersections who are responsible for the success of IDENTITY GUARD® and KID SURE[SM], including Gillian Osborne-Stocker, Begench Atayev, Lindsey George, Sandy Miller, Laurie Kjersgaard, Darren Goldberg, Andy Green, Christy Newman, Taruna Bajaj, Cathleen Karlsson-Shulsinger, Jonathan Garces, Dora Holdarova, Liz Riedl,

Kristin Carlson, Melvin Ng and the entire Solutions Delivery team, Andy Gerry and the entire Operations team, Patti Stiffler and the entire Customer Care team, and the teams of Pete Enghauser, Eric Miller, Joe Vacca, Madalyn Behneman, Tim Walston, and William Fong.

Steve and I are also very grateful to the victims of identity theft who were willing to share their stories with us. Their desire to be involved in this book helped us paint a more complete picture and get us one step closer to ending child identity theft. To them, we express our heartfelt thanks.

We'd also like to thank our friends who we have met through the Children's Miracle Network Hospitals, especially Brian Hazlegren, LaMar Williams, Patricia Jasper-Zellner, John Lauck, Steve Young, and John Schneider for their support of our mutual commitment to kids from the beginning, and to their long-time supporter, Mary Lou Retton. These people and the others at CMNH inspire us with the work they do to help millions of children across this country.

On a practical level, we are very appreciative of the work of our publishing team – Rebecca Bly, Ann Alger, and Karen Burton – who were all tremendously helpful in bringing this book to life. We also received exceptional advice from Steve and Bill Harrison, Jack Canfield, Martha Bullen, and Stephen Harkins. We could have written a book without them, but it certainly would not have been this good.

The team at Meredith Corporation has also been extremely helpful in the planning and launch of the book, especially J.R. McCabe, Danielle Dardashti, Chuck Hajj, and Howard Rosenstein. Their guidance and perspective on parents has contributed immensely to this project. We'd also like to acknowledge all of the mom bloggers who helped us craft our message, especially Amy Lupold-Bair at Resourceful Mommy Media and Beth Feldman at RoleMommy.com. We hope our book makes you proud and helps the millions of parents who rely on your shows, sites, and magazines.

On a more personal note, when I told Steve that I wanted to write a book, I had no idea of the amount of time and effort it was going to take. As it is, my career requires that I spend a good deal of time away from my family – and the writing of this book exacerbated that reality.

I'd therefore like to thank Danielle, my beautiful wife, for her patience, love, and support throughout all the late nights and early mornings. I couldn't have done this without her. My amazing daughters, Emily and Chase, have been an inspiration from the moment that I became a parent – a moment that no parent ever forgets. Without them, I wouldn't have been able to provide the real-world perspectives described in this book. They are my greatest gifts, and keeping them safe is just one way to show my gratitude for all the happiness that they bring.

Last, but certainly not least, I want to thank my Mom and Dad. They have been my role models throughout my life. They showed me the value of a strong family, strong work-ethic, and the importance of giving back. To them, I am the most grateful.

Joe Mason
Haymarket, VA

MISSION
STATEMENT

Our mission is simple. We want to End Child Identity Theft. And we won't settle for less. There are no gimmicks, no Social Security numbers scrawled on city busses, no hype. Just the sincere hope that this Virginia dad can make a difference in this crazy world. We have seen, the devastation child identity theft can cause and to it we say – NO MORE.

We can end child ID theft. It may take an act of Congress, but by raising awareness about this issue, it can happen. In the meantime, we are committed to spreading information and technology that protects kids' from this growing crime. This book, the education program we have created which the book supports and our KID SURE[SM] *child identity theft service are some of the ways we are fighting for kids.*

We can do more to protect our kids—as parents and as a nation. This book is a call to arms for both. We hope you will join us.

BANKRUPT AT BIRTH

WHY CHILD ID THEFT IS ON THE RISE AND HOW IT'S HAPPENING UNDER PARENTS' NOSES

TABLE OF CONTENTS

FOREWORD

You probably remember me from gymnastics and the Olympics and my various television appearances since. Even though at times it seems like only yesterday, 1984 in Los Angeles was a long time ago, and today my life revolves around my four daughters, and my husband, Shannon. I come from a large family, and now I have my own large family. Needless to say, my life has long revolved around children, and I am a mother first and a personality second—a distant second.

My interest in children, and particularly sick children, drew me to the Children's Miracle Network Hospitals more than 20 years ago. I have watched CMNH grow into one of North America's leading children's charities, and supporter of children's hospitals nationwide. Did you know that CMNH has raised more than $4.3 billion with that money going to local children's hospitals?

My regard for children, and my concern for my four daughters, is what drew me to this book. The growth of child identity theft is nothing short of shocking. As you will read, there is a danger to children—my children and your children—one that could ruin their reputations and their abilities to start a happy economic life. Child identity theft is endangering children all across America.

The statistics are already overwhelming and they just continue to grow. The Justice Department's Bureau of Justice Statistics is reporting that millions of young persons, representing five percent of all Americans age 16 or older, have already become the victims of identity theft. The U.S. Federal Trade Commission expects to receive upward of 18,000 formal complaints of child identity theft in 2012. One well-regarded study estimates that 10 percent of children have or will become victims of identity theft.

That is why I am happy to lend my name to an effort to first educating the parents of America to this growing plague that so many parents might not even know is endangering their children, and then to begin a campaign to protect all kids from child identity theft.

As a mother, my life has always been dedicated to my children. When I see some of the frightening stories you will read in the coming pages, I am naturally concerned, and I am concerned for your children also.

I believe that Steve Schwartz and Joe Mason are taking a leadership role in starting a national movement to enlist other parents like us to fight against this growing tide.

I hope you too will listen to what follows and that you too will join this crusade to wipe out identity theft just as you would to end any sort of diseases that afflict children.

Olympic Champion &
Children's Miracle Network Hospitals Board Member,
Mary Lou Retton

INTRODUCTION

If you're reading this book, chances are that you're a parent. And, as a parent, worrying about the well-being of your child comes naturally.

You are always looking out for your child's safety and wellness. And, depending on their age, you worry about more specific things—if they will be injured playing outside, as they go off to school and spend the day out of your sight going to class and interacting with other children. Then you worry about their driving or being driven by a friend. Finally, when they go off to college, you have a whole new world of worries.

We know this, because we are parents, too. We share these same concerns and constant struggles to ensure our children are safe and protected.

Amid all this, many of us have not been looking at whether our children's identities might be stolen, and what the ramifications of identity theft can be on their futures. If you're like the hundreds of other parents we've talked to about this, you've probably never even heard of child identity theft.

We are both fathers of school-aged children and often find ourselves in a social setting with other parents or at a school function and are asked what we do for a living. The answer—and the following conversation—inevitably turns to the growing epidemic of child identity theft. And, almost without exception, we are met with blank looks, and with a range of responses that all come down to no former knowledge of the subject.

You're probably aware of identity theft—the fraudulent use of another person's private information—is usually for financial gain. You may have worried about someone stealing your identity to use your credit cards or withdraw money from your bank account. You might even have gone the next step to set up safeguards to prevent your becoming a victim. If you have, then good for you.

But have you worried about your child's identity? Most parents never do because, after all, what on earth could a thief do with your child's information? You may think because your child has never applied for credit or opened a bank account that their information has no value to an identity thief.

In very simple terms, a child's identity—e.g. their name, Social Security number, and date of birth—can easily wind up in the wrong hands. Just think about how much information you've provided about your child to their schools, hospitals, pharmacies, or sports teams. On the surface, this is all very common and, in most cases, very legitimate. But, if this information winds up in the wrong hands, it can lead to unauthorized bank accounts, credit files, and "synthetic identities"—all using your child's information for someone else's gain.

If the statistics coming out are accurate—and we will look at some data from the Federal Trade Commission and private research companies such as Javelin—you probably have not taken the subject as seriously as you should. This is precisely why I've written this book: To help educate you to the problem and provide guidance and tools to protect your kids from identity theft.

Late in the summer of 2011, the Federal Trade Commission held a first-of-its-kind, full-day forum on child identity theft, which it aptly called "Stolen Futures." The statistics presented were shocking, especially when recognizing that government statistics typically lag several calendar years behind the present. For example, the Justice Department's Bureau of Justice Statistics reported that 11.7 million young persons, representing five percent of all Americans age 16 or older, were victims of identity theft during a two-year period ending in 2008. The Federal Trade Commission itself reported that in 2006, there were more than 10,000 identity-theft complaints filed involving victims who were under the age of 18. This is up from 6,500 cases in 2003. Based on the rate of increase, the Federal Trade Commission expects to receive upward of 18,000 formal complaints of child identity theft in 2012.

A well-regarded recent academic study, from Carnegie Mellon's CyLab, estimates that 10 percent of children have or will become victims of identity theft.

The CyLab study involved examining the records of 42,232 children (age 18 and under) in the U.S during 2009–2010. It found 4,311 (10.2 percent) of the children studied had their Social Security numbers used by other people. Of those, 76 percent involved malicious fraud, 24 percent were cases of accidental mixed credit file information. The study found that "Child IDs were used to purchase homes and automobiles, open credit card accounts, secure employment and obtain driver's licenses. The largest fraud ($725,000) was committed against a 16-year-old girl. The youngest victim was five months old; 303 victims were under the age of five."

I came to learn about this problem through my work as an executive at Intersections Inc., a company that has protected the identities of over 34 million Americans from theft. The disconnect between the explosive growth of child identity theft and the general public's awareness has become increasingly apparent to us and with the help of my colleague Steve Schwartz, I wanted to do something. I run the IDENTITYGUARD.COM brand for Intersections and it's there we get to test our new products. About a year ago, we were able to take our concerns and the recent research to create KID SURE[SM]. KID SURE[SM] provides helps parents protect their child becoming a victim of identity theft.

As a parent, I didn't want KID SURE[SM] to be just another product. We realized child identity theft was a problem that needed a voice. For us, ending child identity theft is a passion—whether it's through education, advocacy, or our technology. As a company, we are commited to going far beyond the limits of traditional marketing to empower parents to protect their kid's most valuable asset—their identity.

In early 2012, two things crossed our desks that had a profound impact on our thinking about child identity theft. The first is Javelin Strategy and Research's 2012 Identity Fraud Survey Report.[1] Each year since 2005, Javelin has conducted an in-depth look at identity theft, and this latest report issued in February found that identity fraud jumped 13 percent in 2011, affecting 11.6 million adults and costing victims untold millions of dollars.

The second item is from the Federal Trade Commission, specifically their annual compilation of the complaints it receives from consumers. In 2011, and for an amazing 12th year in a row, identity theft complaints topped the list. Of more than 1.8 million consumer complaints filed with the Federal Trade Commission in 2011, 15 percent were identity theft complaints.

These two reports are only the latest evidence as to the how insidious the problem of identity theft has become. Day in and day out, we are dedicated to helping people avoid identity theft and, all too often, to recover their identities, credit ratings, and overall peace of mind.

In the pages that follow, I'll describe the problem of identity theft and more specifically how it affects children. I'll tell you what to look for and help your family avoid the pitfalls, as well as provide guidance on how to recover should you find yourself on the wrong side of these statistics.

Additionally, I'll provide resources for what to do and how to recover should this happen to you.

Every day at Intersections, we deal with identity theft and its aftermath and how it can change and shatter lives. Hopefully, by sharing our experience, we can help you to recognize the dangers your children face and guard against those dangers or recover if it's happened to you.

My intent is that this book will educate and provide support for parents as well as have a positive impact toward ending child identity theft. I'll share what I have learned about child identity theft, and later about how I go about protecting my own kids. It is not my intent to scare parents. Instead, my aim is to accomplish three things:

1. to alert you to a very real danger that you may not have previously considered,

2. to assure you that there is something you can and should do about it; and

3. to enlist your support, along with other parents, to help stamp out this very real danger to our kids.

Joe Mason
Chantilly, VA
July 2012

CHAPTER ONE:

THE HIDDEN EPIDEMIC

When I was growing up, things were different, very different. I'm sure you can say the same. And, like any other parent, I've tried to instill strong values in my children, sometimes even wanting to remind them that "I used to walk to school, uphill, both ways!" Well, that's not really true. I rode a school bus. But, things were different back when we were growing up. Forty years ago, I don't think our parents thought much about car seat safety or texting or the Internet or social media or cyber-bullying. In fact, I'm sure of it.

Contrasting "back then" to today, the differences are extreme. Today, we spend a fortune on child safety seats and athletic gear, and woe is the parent whose child is not buckled in properly or whose child doesn't have the right protective gear. When I was a kid, the age that my kids are now, my parents didn't think much about this stuff, and thought it was just fine to be toted around in the back of my great uncle's pickup truck. You probably have similar memories. No one thought much about safety and security—other than the school's favorite "Stop, drop, and roll" drill—which was just fun to do.

In those days, everything was so literal and visual, but today things have changed so much, and so many of the dangers faced by our kids are hidden. If all we had to tell our children is "don't talk to strangers," life would still be simple. But now they are growing up in a world of cyber-crime, of almost previously unimagined technology and now exploding social media.

Many parents don't yet realize that a great danger their children face today is child identity theft. That is why Steve and I have undertaken this book, to make parents more aware of the danger and to tell them what they can do to protect their kids from this very modern danger.

So first let's look at exactly what child identity theft is. You can then begin to see how vulnerable our kids are. The times have changed, but the instinct and passion to protect our kids have not.

You are not alone if you have never considered the threat child identity theft poses to your children; instead, you are among the vast majority. When I bring up the subject with any group of parents, I usually get blank stares in return. It appears that a high percentage of parents have never considered identity theft as it might relate to their own children.

Despite growing at an almost exponential rate, child identity theft was not widely recognized until about 2005 when comprehensive data on it first began to be compiled. What follows is a reality we are exposed to daily in our work with those who've been victims of identity theft.

TYPES OF IDENTITY THEFT

The Identity Theft Resource Center, a non-profit organization based in San Diego, sub-divides identity theft into five categories[1]:

1. Criminal Identity Theft—Posing as another person when apprehended for a crime.

2. Financial Identity Theft—Using another's identity to obtain credit, goods, and services.

3. Identity Cloning—Using another's information to assume his or her identity in daily life.

4. Medical Identity—Theft using another's identity and insurance information to obtain medical care or drugs.

5. Child Identity Theft—Using a child's Social Security number or whole identity for financial gain.

It is this last category that frightens us the most. According to the Federal Trade Commission, child identity theft appears to be the fastest-growing type of identity theft.

LONG-TERM REPERCUSSIONS

Often, the first time a child or parent becomes aware that the child's identity has been stolen occurs when the child attempts their first credit transaction—perhaps purchasing a cell phone or setting up an online account in their own name, applying for college financial aid, or getting that first job, one that requires a background check, credit report and drug test—as almost all do these days.

Most importantly, the repercussions of child identity theft can ultimately "catch up" to the child when he or she becomes an adult. In other words, child identity theft is not a single event that's here today and gone tomorrow. Unfortunately, its effects can linger for years as the following examples illustrate.

Axton Betz never suspected she had a problem until the day she rented her first off-campus apartment in West Lafayette, Indiana. The power company told her she needed to pay a $100 deposit to turn on the electricity. Betz, 19 at the time, assumed they required the deposit because she had no credit history. But, for safe measure, she requested a copy of her credit report.[2]

"I thought it would be just one page on student loans," Betz says. Instead, she found 10 pages of very negative payment records including defaulted credit cards. According to the credit rating bureaus she was thousands of dollars in debt as shown by page after page of open and delinquent accounts.

"I was devastated," said Betz.

Betz says a thief somehow got hold of her Social Security number and those of her parents when she was 11 and used her identity to open account after account. This had happened years back. "I was just a kid growing up in the Indiana countryside. I didn't think about money and credit. I didn't even have a credit card," Axton recalls.

"It's been life-changing and life-defining," said Betz. "It's taken almost half my life to clear this up. "I'm always wondering when is the next collection letter going to arrive, when is the next court summons going to arrive."

Even after Axton tried to convince landlords that the person on the credit reports wasn't her, she was looked at as a credit risk and therefore had to pay sizable cash security deposits to rent an apartment and to get the lights turned on. Similarly, the lowest car loan rate she could get was 18 percent and the lowest credit card interest rate she could get was 29 percent.

In a very real sense, a thief stole her early adult years and turned them into a financial nightmare.

Axton Betz, however, didn't let the thieves completely ruin her future and instead turned lemons into lemonade. She has her doctorate in Human Development and Family Studies and her dissertation is a study on adult and child identity theft victims. Her research has already won her awards and she speaks to groups on the dangers of child identity theft.

Zach Friesen has a very similar story to tell.[3]

When Zach applied for his first job at age 17, a part-time job while he went to school, he learned that apparently he had bought a houseboat for $40,000 when he was seven years old, and then later had defaulted on the loan. His credit was shot and he struggled getting a job and student loans.

He and his mother struggled to clear his name. They spent countless hours and more than a $1,000. Eventually, they thought they were successful, but Zach found out that a decade-long negative credit history is something you can't just get rid of.

"My credit score is very, very bad, as you can imagine $40,000 in debt over the course of ten years could do," Friesen says. "Now, even though I cleared my name, that didn't clear the negative score that I got."

He and his mother have struggled to figure out how his identity was stolen. Given the timeframe during which it happened, the only thing they can come up with is that when Zach visited his pediatrician his Social Security number was being used as an identifier. Like most parents, his mother would sign him in on the office sign-in sheet using his name and Social Security number.

Like Axton, in the example above, Zach has also turned this negative experience into a positive one by helping to educate others. He has been hired by Qwest Communications who has sent him out to speak to more than 200 high schools about identity theft and how students can protect themselves.

> "I just really want kids to walk away with the understanding of what identity theft is—how to prevent it from happening and what to do if it does—because teens and young children are being targeted more than anyone in America."

These cases show how what might be thought of as a relatively simple case of child identity theft—e.g. someone using your identity to start a utility account or to rent an apartment—can turn into more than a decade of turmoil.

What happened to Derek Jones of Reidsville, NC, and his seven-year-old son, is another modern-day example of child identity theft.[4]

Jones had his local tax preparer finish his 2011 tax return, which listed his son as a dependent and therefore worthy of an exemption. The preparer tried to file the return electronically. It was rejected. A mistake certainly. So she put it through again. Rejected again. A call was made to IRS and the reason for the rejection was someone had already put through a return listing his son's name, date of birth, and Social Security number. Someone had stolen his child's identity.

Jones and the preparer did the only thing they felt was open to them. They removed the boy from the return and refiled it, taking the financial hit from the loss of a deduction.

"They told me that they couldn't do it unless I took his name off because somebody had already used his Social Security number for their filing," Jones told a local television station. "He's only seven. It's not like he's got bank accounts or money or anything, but that's not even the issue. They know where he lives, and they've just got all of his information right there."

Actually, Jones did have other options. As you will see later, what happened to him, while shocking to him, is far from shocking to the IRS. Instead of simply filing without the exemption, Jones should have filed a paper return, included a letter detailing the situation along with a copy of his son's birth certificate and proof that he is the custodial parent, and asked that the return and the documentation be forwarded to the IRS's local identity theft unit.

Yes, the IRS has seen so many of these cases. They now number in the tens of thousands, and identity theft units to investigate them have been established across the nation.

Also, as you will see in the pages that follow, Jones should have taken a number of additional steps to ensure his son's identity has not also been used by the scammer in additional ways.

As we will shortly see, stealing an identity and especially a child's identity (or at least temporarily borrowing one) is all too easy.

SOME STATISTICS

As I previously noted, the Federal Trade Commission listed identity theft as the most reported complaint—for the fourth year in a row.

Florida is the state with the highest per capita rate of reported identity theft complaints, followed by Georgia and California. If you live in Maine, South Dakota or North Dakota, you may be lucky. Based on consumer complaints received, they were least likely places for identity theft.

The Federal Trade Commission says based on its data and the complaints it is getting, the main use of a stolen identity appears to be government documents/ benefits fraud. Specifically, 27 percent of all complaints involved criminals filing bogus tax returns (in someone else's name) hoping to cash in on the tax refund. This includes phony tax returns seeking refunds (27 percent), followed by credit card fraud (14 percent), phone or utilities fraud (13 percent) and bank fraud (9 percent). Other significant categories of identity theft reported by victims were employment fraud (8 percent) and loan fraud (3 percent). It's important to note that these statistics are based on self-reported cases. So we expect the real numbers to be even higher, specifically for cases related to child identity theft. As the above examples illustrate, detecting the crime when it occurs rarely happens. Typically, child identity theft is detected once the child becomes an adult, and needs credit either for a cell phone, student loan, car, or an apartment. Since most kids don't have or need credit until adulthood, that's when identity theft is most often detected. This is why it's so important for parents take the steps now to protect their children.

At the Federal Trade Commission symposium "Stolen Futures," the Carnegie Mellon's CyLab examination of more than 42,000 children found that over 10 percent of those who had their Social Security numbers used found that the thief might have been involved in what we call "friendly fraud"—a member of their own families or household. This type of theft is also referred to as "familial" or "inter-generational" identity theft.

In other instances, the thief might be a total stranger, or a group of total strangers. In a surprising number of cases, a young person's stolen identity may be in use by multiple crooks.

What is particularly insidious about child identity theft is the fact it can go on for years without the victim or the victim's parents having any indication that something has happened or is happening.

The consequences of child ID theft are staggering.
Get the facts you need to know. Go to
www.BankruptAtBirthBook.com
to download
The Quick Start Guide to Child ID Theft.

THE HIDDEN EPIDEMIC

Steven Toporoff, an attorney with the Division of Privacy and Identity Protection at the Federal Trade Commission told last summer's symposium that child identity theft is a bigger problem than most people realize, and said a lack of data makes it hard to raise awareness about the swiftly growing crime. "It's completely underreported because parents in many instances have no suspicion that their child's identity has been taken. Children certainly don't know," Toporoff says. "While we don't know how prevalent it is, it can be devastating when it happens to a particular family."[5]

Corbin Russell, of Harvard, Nebraska faces perhaps an extreme manifestation of this problem. He just graduated from Harvard High School but can't go onto college because he can't get a loan or loan guarantee because he is supposedly... dead.[6]

According to local media reports, Corbin was surprised by his death because he feels fine, as healthy as a normal 18-year-old.

It appears that someone stole Corbin's Social Security number and it was used in a death benefit claim for a man who died in January 2010 in South Carolina.

Corbin told reporters he learned of the problem when he tried to get a car loan. "After they ran a credit check score, it came back with a couple of alerts," he said. "I had been dead for the past couple of years."

He and his mother Monica say his college scholarship applications have been rejected because of the flagged credit reports, and a valid and unchallenged Social Security number is necessary to seek student loans.

Fixing it is taking time, a lot of time. "In some cases it's taken two years, and he can't go to college until it's fixed," Monica told reporters.

She worries if her son is forced to sit out two years, he will lose his desire to go to college.

This dreadful scenario, an inability to qualify for a student loan because of a negative credit report all caused by identity theft, will play out in homes throughout America this year.

SYNTHETIC IDENTITY THEFT

When most people think of ID theft they picture those old TV commercials of the guy on the tractor dressed as a woman. What they are imaging is when someone "takes over" another name and SSN and uses it as their own. This is the type of ID theft you might be able to track down through a traditional credit report, but the problem for kids is that it is uncommon, though not unheard of, for a scammer to completely assume a child's identity—that is his or her entire name and Social Security number.

Instead, what usually occurs is called "synthetic identity theft," in which an identity is essentially fabricated usually by combining a real Social Security number—your son or daughter's—with a fabricated name or sometimes with the real name of the scammer.

Too often—in fact a majority of the time—the first time a child or parent becomes aware that the child's Social Security number has been stolen is when the child attempts their first credit transaction such as applying for financial aid, purchasing a cell phone, buying a car, or applying for a job that requires a credit check or background investigation.

ACCIDENTAL IDENTITY THEFT

There is another situation that deserves a mention—what might be called inadvertent or accidental identity theft. Some people simply misremember their Social Security numbers. Or, sometimes Social Security numbers are mis-keyed on a loan form or some other credit record. Numbers are accidentally transposed or a wrong key is hit, and an identity becomes established under what is essentially a wrong Social Security number.

We have seen it happen and the result is usually benign. A young person finds when they first apply for credit that a file already exists. There may be a file, but it shows good credit. The person whose file it is can be quickly contacted and the discrepancy corrected. It becomes a no- harm, no-foul situation. It may take some effort to correct the mistake, but such mistakes are correctable. However, questions still linger.

After graduating college in 2001, Stephanie McManis applied for her first credit card, but was rejected. Only after she requested her credit report did she learn that someone else had used her identity since she was 12 years old, she said. Her credit report was "inches thick," she said, filled with unpaid mortgages, car loans, cell phone contracts, and credit card debt.[7]

McManis filed a report with her local police department and authorities tracked down the woman who was using her identity and living just a few hours away in Avon, Ohio, just west of Cleveland. Avon Police, who investigated the case, said the Social Security numbers of the two women are one digit off, and he believed the confusion was caused by "nothing more than a clerical error" by someone at a credit agency, not identity theft.

But the chore came in unraveling the two identities and then a question remained: clerical error/accident or actual identity theft. If it was an honest mistake, why did the woman continue to use McManis' Social Security number even after being contacted?

Even in cases where theft might seem accidental, it is never a mistake to continue to follow-up and be sure that identity theft is not in the makings.

WARNING SIGNS

Think about this: If a thief goes after a random adult identity, such an identity may already have a tarnished credit record, for example. Or, it may be actively monitored for misuse. In such cases, there's simply no value for the thief. On the other hand, a child's identity will seldom have any history—negative or positive—and chances are good that it's not being actively monitored either. A child's identity is new and untarnished—and the icing on the cake to the scammer is that it's very unlikely that it's being monitored either. It's no wonder, then, that children are more likely to have their identities stolen than adults.

If you're lucky, there may be warning signs. Your child may start getting unsolicited offers for credit cards. If this happens to your child, take this as an indication that something could be seriously wrong. The answer may be that a credit file or a marketing list exists somewhere on your child. Another warning sign is if a collection agency tries to collect on a debt related to your child. In more serious cases, you may end up at the emergency room only to find out your child has a long health record on file with Medicaid or Medicare or with a major health insurer. Or, one of the most ominous warning signs can be taking your teenager down for a driver's test and first license only to realize she is leaving the DMV in handcuffs on an outstanding warrant—or, if you're lucky, instead of being handcuffed, she is just handed a bill for hundreds of dollars in unpaid tickets.

While seemingly outlandish, these are not unheard-of scenarios. They are happening with appalling regularity. By now, your understanding of the threat that identity theft poses to your child has probably grown. I am hoping you'll agree that child identity theft should be a major concern to every parent. In the next chapter we'll explain how we got here, why child ID theft is on the rise, and begin to give you a sense of just how deep the roots of the problem run.

CHAPTER TWO:

A BRIEF HISTORY OF THE SOCIAL SECURITY NUMBER

I keep coming back to the central fact that, at the heart of child identity theft—the greatest threat your son or daughter faces—is their Social Security number. The Social Security Administration will shout from the roof tops that the number they issue is not now, nor was it ever intended to be, a national identity number for every individual. But over the years, it has become a de facto national identification number, which is why it's at the heart of most identity theft.

In the United States, the nine-digit Social Security number is available to U.S. citizens, permanent residents and temporary residents in the country who are here under the various visa programs that allow for legal employment. Ever since the Social Security program was started in 1935 as a central part of President Franklin Roosevelt's New Deal social program, these numbers are issued upon request with their primary purpose to track individuals for Social Security benefit purposes. Within three months of the start of the program, 25 million numbers had been issued.

If that is where the use of the Social Security number had remained (i.e. simply for tracking Social Security benefits), identity theft would be a relatively minor statistic on the crime blotter today. A stolen Social Security number would be of value to an undocumented alien looking for work, but that would be about it. But how things have changed since the Social Security program started 85-plus years ago.

Let's go all the way back to 1935 and look at the original Social Security Act. That law specifically limited the use of the Social Security number to direct Social Security purposes. That's the way things stayed, until as recently as the 1960s.

The IRS began to complain. It needed some universal way of easily identifying taxpayers and common names did not work because, well, how many John Smiths file tax returns each year? The IRS said the cost and time to develop a universal taxpayer identification number system would be exorbitant, especially in light of the fact, a dandy system already existed which met virtually all of their needs at NO cost. That system is known as the Social Security system. So "unofficially," in 1962, the IRS began using Social Security numbers as taxpayer identification numbers even though, technically, they were in apparent violation of the letter of the original Social Security law. Starting in the 1962 tax year, the IRS required taxpayers to list their Social Security numbers on their returns, and on all tax documents and communications.

Then the Pentagon got into the act, also arguing that it did not want to reinvent the wheel, so to speak and, beginning in 1969, the Social Security number started to be used as the official identification number for all in the military.

The unofficial–official use of the Social Security number by IRS continued until the mid-1970s when Congress agreed in the Tax Reform Act of 1976 to amend the Internal Revenue Code to provide that the Social Security number be used as the tax identification number for all tax purposes. While they were at it, after a bit of arm twisting by the states, Congress allowed states to use Social Security numbers in their own tax systems, for general public assistance programs and for driver's licenses or motor vehicle registration.

The Social Security Administration was not happy, but the flood gates were now opened. Through the 1980s and into the 1990s various laws were passed not only allowing the more widespread use of the Social Security number but actually requiring its use in applying for and obtaining various kinds of federally guaranteed loans and grants including student loans and in massive federal programs including Medicare and Medicaid. From time to time, Congress has talked about limiting the use of Social Security numbers, but nothing has come of this, and instead the use has continued to spread. Today, the Social Security number has become a de facto national identity number, and the only reason Congress has not gone the extra step in declaring it so is because of the difficulty in devising a tamper proof, forgery proof, Social Security number-based national identity card, and the objections of many privacy advocates.

ATTAINING SOCIAL SECURITY NUMBERS

One of the most interesting cases I have run across concerns Michelle Dennedy and her daughter Reilly. Ms. Dennedy is not just any civilian. She is highly successful executive who has held positions as the chief privacy officer for Sun Microsystems, vice president for privacy at Oracle Corp, and now chief privacy officer at the security firm McAfee. She has learned that nine-year-old Reilly has had her identity used by scammers not once but twice.[1]

As distressing as this is, it is not all that unusual that once a Social Security number, or a whole identity for that matter, is in circulation, it is used by multiple thieves. But what makes this case interesting, and far from unique, is when one of the scammers began using Reilly's Social Security number.

Michelle looked at the eventual negative credit report she got under Reilly's name and realized some of the accounts went back 12 years. Three years *before Reilly was born!*

How is that possible? The best guess is that more than a decade earlier a scammer had simply made up a Social Security number either by transposing some numbers from an existing Social Security number or making up one from scratch. Then along comes Michelle and her husband, they apply for a number for Reilly, the law of coincidence rears its ugly head, and Reilly is issued the same number that the Social Security Administration correctly believes it has never previously issued.

Is Reilly's case unique? The complicated answer is yes, no, and maybe.

First of all, you will remember we have said the one almost universal fact of child identity theft is that, unless a concerned parent—hopefully by the time you finish reading this book that will describe you—intervenes and intervenes aggressively, it will likely be years before any individual case of child identity theft is discovered. (In what follows, you'll discover the tools to become aggressive in perusing whether your child has already become a victim.) Quite probably, as more and more cases like Reilly's come to light, there will be others, possibly many others, where the Social Security Administration gives a child a "new" Social Security number, and it is later shown that some scammer has already put that number into use, as it was in Reilly's case.

REQUIRING A SOCIAL SECURITY NUMBER FROM BIRTH

There was a time, as recently as the mid-1980s, that young people did not even think about getting a Social Security number until they got a first job and started to have taxes withheld from paychecks.

Up until this time, taxpayers were expected to be truthful in claiming exemptions on their taxes. But, the IRS was sure it was being exposed to widespread fraud wherein taxpayers were claiming children who didn't exist, or children who they were no longer supporting. So the IRS went to Congress and complained and passed the Tax Reform Act of 1986. It required, for the first time, that all dependents over the age of five have their own Social Security numbers in order to be claimed as a dependent.

The IRS knew it was onto something when, the next year, around seven million fewer minor dependents were claimed. The IRS (and members of Congress looking for more revenue) concluded that if requiring Social Security numbers for all claimed dependents over the age of five resulted in washing some seven million dependents out of the system how many of those still left would disappear if they lowered the age of claimed dependents needing a Social Security number to age one.

So Congress jumped on board and, by 1990, the threshold was lowered to one year old, and today is required for all claimed dependents regardless of the child's age.

Since then, parents have often applied for Social Security numbers for their children soon after birth. In fact, starting with a pilot program in New Mexico in 1987, the Social Security Administration made the whole process easier by including forms necessary to obtaining a Social Security number in the paperwork new parents fill out to acquire a birth certificate. Today, in many jurisdictions, such issuance is all but automatic. You fill out the forms in the hospital and, in due course, a copy of the birth certificate will arrive, and soon after your baby's new Social Security card issued by the Social Security Administration.

On its website the Social Security Administration urges all new parents to take advantage of this shortcut. SSA says:

> "You will have an option to complete this request at the hospital when you apply for your baby's birth certificate. The state agency that issues birth certificates will share your child's information with us, and we will mail the Social Security card to you."

HOW SOCIAL SECURITY NUMBERS ARE GENERATED

The Social Security Administration says the calculation of the Social Security number comes down to simple math. The nine-digit Social Security number has already been issued in more than 400 million different sequences. There used to be a formula in how these nine-digit numbers were arrived at: the first three numbers originally represented the state in which a person first applied for a Social Security card, two middle digits, which range from 01 through 99, are simply used to break all the Social Security numbers with the same area number into smaller blocks, and the last four digits run consecutively from 0001 through 9999. This has now changed, and the nine digits are generated randomly with no area bias. The random generated numbers are then checked against already-assigned numbers to prevent duplicates.

It was easy for a criminal to make up a Social Security number using the old formula. But the real irony is that it's not really any harder now. Given the number of numeric possibilities and the number of people who have been issued a Social Security number, the odds are good that if someone makes up a number, it may be a number already in use or one that will be given out in the future. This, of course, is unlike picking numbers for the lottery where the numbers are here today and gone tomorrow. Social Security numbers, by contrast, last during life and after death.

Ms. Dennedy related her experiences at the Federal Trade Commission Child Identity Theft Symposium and told the audience: "All of us have a little bit to do with solving the problem. We are no longer going to passively hand our children over to bad guys who are only focused on exploiting their good names."

CHAPTER THREE:

THE NAKED PUBLIC

I think we all understand why young people feel so invincible. Almost no matter what the danger, the 17 year old thinks, it'll never happen to me. But this feeling of invincibility is not limited to teenagers. In certain areas, adults can be just as naïve. From my experience, identity theft is one of those areas.

This chapter is intended to be a primer. I'll give you the history of identity theft and bring it up to today. My goal, in doing this, is to make you aware of the danger you face and the fact that your information is out there—you are exposed.

I understand that identity theft can feel like global warming—it's too big for you or me to fix so we might as well do nothing. The problem is that with the explosion of technology, your exposure to identity theft is exponential. The terms malware, viruses, keyloggers are all complicated and just plain scary.

My frustration is that people are so naïve and continue to ignore the simple things they can do and should do to prevent becoming a victim. Some say "I avoid technology." Or "I never shop online," and therefore believe they can never become a victim." That ignores the fact that, for the most part, online shopping can be safer than giving your credit card to a waiter in a restaurant.

So come along on a journey where it's my hope you will learn about identity theft in all its manifestations and, in doing so, you will begin make yourself less of a target.

You might think that identity theft is a poor stepchild of the computer era. But the crime is much older than that. Almost as far back as we have recorded history, taking another's identity was accomplished, quickly and finally, by the bad guy simply killing the person whose identity he (or an occasional she) wanted, and then taken possession of what the dead person had owned—be it tangible things like horses, cattle, and money or intangible things like assuming the dead victim's identity for their own gain.

This kind of definitive identity theft was prevalent in the nineteenth century, especially in the era following the Civil War, in what we now call the Wild West.

In the twentieth century, identity theft became, if less deadly, much more insidious and more widespread. A new breed of scammers latched onto identity theft. It was often accomplished by telephone. The telephone would ring and an excited voice would tell you that you have won a sweepstakes, a lottery, a contest you didn't remember entering and the prize would be on its way, but first you needed to provide your address, bank name and account number, and your Social Security number. Such scams continue to this day.

These kinds of phone scams were the forerunners of emails conveying the same thing—that is, an email telling you that you have won something. The sender of this type of email will claim that they are authorized to complete the transaction and to get access to the promised riches, all you have to do is supply "some personal information" and perhaps supply bank account numbers, a small payment to show your good faith. Then, just sit back and wait for the promised riches to flow in.

You've seen these kinds of emails probably all too often, we're sure, and you have always thought to yourself who would be dumb enough to respond. You would be shocked to learn how many people around the world do, and how much is lost to the scammers each year.

DUMPSTER DIVING

Another way scammers got access to personal information in the pre-computer era was through a process called "dumpster diving."

In the old days—that is, if you call the 1950s and 1960s the old days—dumpster diving meant literally that. Scammers would rummage through trash in garbage cans at the curb, or where the activity got its name in dumpsters behind offices and apartment buildings or even in landfills looking for bills or other papers with people's personal information on them. In other words, they would physically attempt to acquire the kind of personal information that would give them access to another person's assets.

There were other ways that schemers latched onto personal information. They would follow postmen and steal the mail being left in outside boxes. For them, a goldmine included bank and credit card statements; monthly bills that included account numbers; occasionally one of those pre-approved credit card new account offers; and the occasional bonanza of a box of new blank checks. Sometimes scammers would go to post offices and file change of address forms to divert mail to new locations accessible to them.

This kind of identity theft still exists today.

Brian Hurley and his neighbors live in the Waterford subdivision in the Chicago suburb of Elgin, Illinois. One night, Brian got a call from a ticket agent at New York's JFK Airport that alerted him to the fact that an individual had purchased an airline ticket there using Hurley's credit card. His identity had been stolen, and he began a months-long odyssey to clear his good credit.[1]

But then in short order Mr. Hurley's neighbors started to come forward saying their identities had been stolen, too. First two, then three, then finally six neighbors were all victims of identity theft.

How did it happen? The most likely answer is it happened the old-fashioned way. In the subdivision every four houses have their mailboxes on a shared post. It is likely someone or some group has been rifling through mail. But investigators also looked into a new modern possibility and are still trying to determine if the half-dozen victims share a common computer node because some or all get their Internet service via their cable TV provider or it could be that someone hacked into their wireless Internet connections.

Sometimes it can be relatively easy to determine where and how identities have been stolen. When police in West Des Moines received complaints from a dozen people that they were victims of identity theft and their credit cards were suddenly being fraudulently used, they immediately looked for some kind of link among them.[2]

The cards themselves had not been lost; they were physically in the possession of their rightful owners. So police began looking at where they had been used most recently before the illegal activity began. What had happened and where it had happened became quickly apparent. All the people who were being victimized had eaten recently at the same local restaurant.

As soon as the police knew how and where, they began working with the restaurant's owners to determine who perpetrated the crime, which remains unsolved.

Things were not as easy for authorities, local and federal, in Teaneck, New Jersey. The township of about 40,000 residents outside New York City now has almost 200 reported cases of identity theft. There credit card numbers have been used as locally in New York and as far away as Miami and the West Coast.[3]

So far, police are stumped trying to find a common causality linking all the victims. At first there was a suspicion that many had used the cards in a cluster of local shops, but other victims have come forward who have never set foot in those shops. Police suspected some form of dumpster diving but some victims swear they shred every piece of personal mail—bills, statements, receipts—before disposing of them. They are looking into the Internet Service Providers (ISPs) used by the victims. Or, could their mail have been stolen at some central sorting facility? So far, police have a number of theories, but few answers.

IDENTITY THEFT—A COMPLEX CRIME

As identity theft has become more prevalent, it has become more complex, and as it has become more complex, so has the prosecution of it become more complex.

Take the case of an Oakfield, New York woman, Gail P. Rumble, (aka Gail P. Montondo according to court records) who was indicted for stealing her son's and her ex-husband's identities in order to obtain cable, electric, and natural gas services.[4]

She faced a 10-count indictment filed in Genesee County Court. She was charged under New York State law with two counts of second-degree identity theft, three counts of third-degree identity theft, and five counts of second-degree criminal impersonation. Second degree, third degree, identity theft, criminal impersonation; what's the difference?

To start with, the degree of the crime is based on the amount of money that has been obtained illegally. In New York, stealing up to $200 is third degree. Two-hundred dollars to $500 is second degree. Above $500 is first degree. The difference is that third degree is a misdemeanor, second degree and first degree are felonies, and all three classifications carry different penalties. First degree and second degree usually carry mandatory jail time.

In New York, criminal impersonation is a set of laws that existed before the dawn of identity theft laws and covers an instance when a defendant impersonates another person with the intent to obtain a particular benefit. It is used today mainly in situations where there is an unsuccessful attempt that falls outside the identity theft statutes.

These days, you often see that persons charged with the crime of "aggravated identity theft." This came about in 2004, when Congress enacted the "Identity Theft Penalty Enhancement Act." The law increased criminal penalties for identity theft and conceived, for the first time, the crime of "aggravated identity theft." By and large, it refers to the use of identity theft to commit a whole list of crimes starting with terrorism and then going through a whole laundry list of federal criminal statutes including trying to defraud the federal government.

Federal persecutors always charge aggravated identity theft in false income tax filing cases. They also seem to charge it in most other cases, and they use it because it carries a stiffer penalty (starting with a mandatory two years) than other forms of identity theft.

Today, virtually every state has identity theft laws that parallel New York's with minor differences in dollar amounts and penalties. Most states have also added the crime of aggravated identity theft to their laws using wording close to the federal statute.

The good news for all of us is that nationwide prosecutors are recognizing the problem identity theft has become and are starting to more vigorously go after offenders.

COMPUTER-ERA IDENTITY THEFT

The dawning of the computer era has brought, if not a new kind of identity theft, one that uses technology to obtain and use other people's personal information for nefarious purposes. The underlying crime has not changed—that is, to get personal information and use that information fraudulently. With technology and the explosive growth of social media, identity theft has been made more widespread and much easier for thieves.

PHISHING, VISHING, AND SMISHING

Today's thieves may get the information they use directly from the victim by convincing them to divulge it. The traditional way was to call a potential victim on the phone and say they had won a prize. The new-age information thief uses what is now called "phishing"—computer communications pretending to be a bank, credit card company, Internet service provider, business, governmental agency including the IRS, or some other trusted source, and saying the information is needed.

Some phishing scams can get very sophisticated. The scam email might contain an urgent message about a bank account problem and urge the recipient to call a toll-free number. That number will request personal information in a way anyone calling their bank has heard many times before, but it will be a fake automated system being run by the scammers.

Another phishing scam that is rampant is being called the jury duty scam. It's amazingly simple and amazingly effective. The phone rings, and it's the sherriff's office, or maybe the local "jury commissioner" informing you that an arrest warrant has or will be issued for you for failure to respond to a summons for jury duty. Wait a minute, you plead, and you've never received any summons. Maybe it's an error, says the voice on the other end of the phone. Give me your full name, address, date of birth, and Social Security number, and I will check these against the files to see if possibly an error has been made on our end. We'll get back to you, he says. No he won't, and just like that, you've had your identity stolen.

Nowadays, phishing has been joined in the lexicon by "vishing" (using voice recording systems) and "smishing" (combining SMS and phishing—SMS being the technology that delivers text messages to cellphones) and "spearphishing" (phishing against a small group of selected targets who are more likely to be attracted such as members of an organization or club).

Usually, the information inquiry comes in the form of a request for information verification. One that has been termed "very effective" by authorities is a very official-looking email purportedly from the Internal Revenue Service asking you to confirm among other things your Social Security number and your banking affiliation and account number (so they can "process your refund without delay"). If it's from the "IRS," many people don't give a second thought to replying, this despite the fact that the IRS makes numerous public statements that they will never send out emails asking for such information.

A significant number of phishing scams involve emails purportedly from consumer giant Walmart offering Walmart gift cards to respondents. The scam, in a warning posted by Walmart on its website, evolves like this.

Consumers either receive a spam email or come across a web advertisement or website offering a Walmart or other well-known gift card worth a large amount of money. The consumer is taken to a website that is has branding that makes it appear to be a legitimate merchant (ex: Walmart), there the consumer will be asked to enter an email address and other personal contact information; including address and phone number. If you respond, you likely have had your identity stolen.

Spearphishing is an especially effective way of exploiting your own social media information against you. If you have given out too much information about yourself perhaps on Twitter or Facebook, cyber crooks can make some informed guesses as to what your interests are or what you do for a living. Then, they may target you with an email that may appear to have been sent by a friend or business colleague and might, for instance, send a link to a conference on a topic that the scammer has learned would be of interest to you, or tell you to check out a report or news story on a topic they've gleaned from your postings. Their goal is to get you to click onto a malicious attachment or get you to link to a false website where they can attempt to steal personal information from you.

In another recent incident, scammers saying they were from Washington went door to door in a small northeast Georgia community of Elberton asking residents for information to facilitate their receiving direct stimulus funds. More than 100 residents of the town ended up having their identities stolen.[5]

It's easier and more efficient, however, to scam in bulk. The scammers have found that if they buy a list of 100,000 email addresses, and send out a blanket request pretending to be a well-known bank, they will hit hundreds of people who use that particular bank and some number of them will fall for the official-looking requests and will provide the information.

You've probably had such phony requests pop into your email boxes and you've deleted them without much thought. If you have thought about them you probably have wondered how anyone could fall for them. The trouble is that many consumers still do respond, thereby fueling the fire for identity thieves.

As an aside, our favorite recent email of this kind purports to be from the wife of a bank official in Qatar who, unbeknownst to him, has caught her husband cheating. Her husband, she relates, has already looted an inactive account at his bank for millions and deposited into a joint account she has access to.

She needs to get that money out of the joint account and to a safe place very quickly so she can dump her wandering husband and disappear. Won't you help her out by sending your banking information so she can move the hot money before her husband moves it himself?

Because enough people respond to such stories, phishing remains a very lucrative activity. In 2005, for example, federal police in Brazil arrested Valdir Paulo de Almeida, the leader of a gang who stole $37 million from his victims' bank accounts using a malicious computer program called a "Trojan horse" that people were tricked into downloading onto their computer via phishing emails.[6] At one point it was estimated this gang was sending out three million phishing emails a day.

Sometimes the scammers are highly sophisticated gangs using the latest in computer techniques to fool their victims. But other times the thieves are teenagers sitting in their bedrooms using their computers to send out random emails looking for the gullible person who will send them credit card numbers they can then use to acquire new sneakers or other goods.

DATA BREACHES

What I find interesting are the numbers of people who fall victim who do not have the slightest idea where the scammers got their vital information. They tell you they are too smart to have fallen victim to any kind of phishing expedition, and they have never given out any personal information in response to an email request.

This is likely true. What they are victims to, most likely, are the increasing numbers of data breaches at companies, organizations, and institutions where very sophisticated computer hackers defeat security programs and gain access to data bases of customers, employees, members, or users.

To our growing dismay, it seems that not a week goes by when another data breach doesn't make headlines. Here are two small examples from one recent week:

A University of Maine computer server was breached by hackers and may have exposed personal information, including credit card and Social Security numbers of students, college officials recently said.[7]

Potentially affected students made purchases through a campus-based computer store at the University of Maine's campus in Orono.

The university said in a news release that the data on the UMaine server breached by hackers included 2,818 "unique identifiers," which may include as many as 435 credit card numbers and 1,175 Social Security numbers.

York County, South Carolina admitted there could be 17,000 potential victims after a security breach. Authorities admitted that a backup web server was breached last and, most disturbingly, the breach was tracked to a suspected hacker overseas.

York County Manager Jim Baker said the overseas hacker could have accessed names and Social Security numbers for the county's current employees and former job applicants.[8]

Actually, even more troubling is the fact that data breaches have become so commonplace that they no longer garner headlines but are instead buried somewhere else in the newspaper or online blog. Last year, the Verizon RISK Team in cooperation with the U.S. Secret Service released a study of data breaches in which personal information was potentially compromised.

This was a follow up by a similar study done two years before, along with an examination of 800 new breaches that had occurred in the interim. Cumulatively, over the seven years these studies were done, the RISK team says more than 1,700 breaches have been examined covering over 900 million compromised records.[9]

I'll give you a moment to contemplate this number—*900 million. How likely is it, you may be asking yourself, or should be asking yourself, that some of your personal information is in the wrong hands?*

A similar study of breaches was conducted by the Identity Theft Resource Center. In the six-year period, 2005 through 2011, the ITRC identified 3,154 reported data breaches in the United States. Of those breaches, more than 511 million consumer records were exposed to the possibility of theft, fraud, or other malicious activity. Do a bit of math—3,154 breaches over a six-year period comes out to 1.4 breaches per day and 233,329 records exposed each and every day during those six years. Even worse, many breaches that occur are untraceable and happen without the knowledge of the data holder. Moreover, even when the owner knows about a data breach, it often goes unreported.[10]

Why they go unreported is pretty obvious. When the fact of the breach becomes public, the lawsuits are seldom far behind. In 2009, Heartland Payment Systems, a major credit card processor suffered a breach that resulted in the exposure of data on 130 million credit cards. A class-action lawsuit was filed alleging that Heartland had negligently failed to protect the personal financial information from disclosure. Heartland settled this suit by depositing $2.4 million in an account to compensate individuals who later would submit claims. Heartland estimated the data breach cost the company upward of $140 million in fines, settlements, legal fees, and lost business.[11]

In 2010, the Federal Trade Commission notified almost 100 corporations and other organizations that sensitive data about customers and/or employees, apparently stored on those companies' and organizations' computer systems is now on file-sharing networks and available to any and all users of those networks.

> "Unfortunately, companies and institutions of all sizes are vulnerable to serious peer-to-peer (P2P)-related breaches, placing consumers' sensitive information at risk," said Federal Trade Commission Chairman, Jon Leibowitz, upon release of these notifications. "For example, we found health-related information, financial records, and drivers' license and Social Security numbers—the kind of information that could lead to identity theft."

Peer-to-peer file sharing allows all users to connect and search for and download shared files. The "peers" in P2P are computer systems connected to each other via the Internet. The only requirement for a computer to be part of a peer-to-peer network is an Internet connection and the proper software.

According to the authoritative Javelin Strategy & Research Study I mentioned earlier, 2011 saw a 67 percent increase in the number of Americans impacted by data breaches as compared to 2010. The study found that victims of data breaches are 9.5 times more likely to be a victim of identity fraud than consumers whose data has never been compromised by a data breach.

Data breaches often come from unscrupulous employees inside the organization. Organized crime and gangs are placing people in lower-level jobs with companies and governmental agencies. These jobs pay little, but offer access to databases rich in personal data—data that can be later sold to a crime ring.

One such instance may have come to light in South Carolina when it was discovered that Christopher Lykes Jr., who was with the state's Health and Human Services Department stole personal information from more than 228,000 Medicaid patients in South Carolina. The information included names, phone numbers, addresses, birth dates, and Medicare ID numbers. Authorities say the employee compiled the data over several months and then sent it to his private email account. He has refused to tell authorities what he planned to do with the information.[12]

What has struck me is how inventive identity thieves have become, and how they can sometimes make do with less information yet are able to steal more and more.

Here is one glaring example of this dismaying and ever-evolving problem. A law-abiding and unaware citizen files his tax return sometime in late March or near the April 15th filing deadline. In due course, a nice letter comes from the Internal Revenue Service asking why you have filed a second return because it processed a return for you in January. It seems that a scammer got just your name and Social Security number and, using just those two pieces of information, filed a phony return requesting and receiving a sizable refund, which was often direct deposited into an equally phony bank account set up specifically to receive the IRS transfer and then drained. Of course, by now the scammer is long gone and the innocent taxpayer has a mess on his hands

THE RAPID RISE OF TAX ID FRAUD

How prevalent is this situation? The IRS reports that in 2010, it uncovered 48,966 cases of "bad" (meaning likely fraudulent) returns. They held back $247 million in refunds being requested in these questionable returns. Last year, in 2011, the number of suspected fraudulent returns jumped to 261,982 and involved $1.4 billion in requested refunds. As of March 9, 2012, more than a month before the end of tax season, the IRS says it has stopped 215,000 questionable returns with $1.15 billion in claimed refunds.

As the IRS's Inspector General told Congress as of December 31, 2011, the IRS's Incident Tracking Report showed that 641,052 taxpayers were affected by identity theft in calendar year 2011. In calendar year 2011, the IRS says it stopped $1.4 billion in refunds from being erroneously sent to identity thieves. Since 2008, the IRS has identified more than 460,000 taxpayers who appear to have had their identities stolen.

The problem is the number of taxpayers filing electronically. Employers are not required to submit copies of withholding statements until March 31 so, with returns filed before that date, the IRS has to take the word of taxpayers as to income earned and taxes withheld. If the IRS begins probing deeper into each electronic return it gets, the whole process of quickly issuing legitimate refunds to taxpayers will slow and cries of outrage will be heard from taxpayers waiting for that money. So, quite often, a refund goes out before it is determined the return is illegitimate.

In the inspector general's report to Congress, he noted that an individual case can take up to a year to unravel. If all refunds in suspected cases were held up, the situation would quickly become untenable. So refunds are withheld usually only in obvious cases.

The filing of fraudulent tax returns seeking refunds has become something of a national epidemic and Tampa, Florida, has become something of a hotbed.

Operation Rainmaker, as federal, state, and local authorities called a yearlong effort by Tampa-area law enforcement agencies and the U.S. Secret Service was able to intercept $100 million in fraudulently filed refunds, and to recover some $5 million in cash, jewelry, cars, and entertainment systems obtained with the proceeds of fraudulent returns. Another $25 million that was paid out by the IRS hasn't been recovered.[13]

Authorities arrested 49 people using people's names, Social Security numbers, and dates of birth to file fraudulent returns electronically. Each return requested a refund that the IRS then issued to a prepaid debit card or by check or direct deposit to a account set up to receive the refund.

As you may already know, the IRS maintains an automated phone system you can call to get the "status" of an already-filed return. The perpetrators in this case would call that line to determine if a return had already been filed in the name of the person they were going to file as.

Several local businesses were also used to launder the stolen money. Nearly $400,000 was seized from the businesses, including $333,000 in federal checks, cash, and money orders.

The suspects had "basically corrupted the online tax-filing system." U.S. Secret Service Special Agent John Joyce said.

According to one account, Tampa police Lt. Mark Scott was one victim. When he tried to file his return, it was rejected because records showed it had already been filed and a refund issued. Scott couldn't help investigate his own identity theft because of taxpayer privacy restrictions in the federal tax code.

"It felt like I was victimized twice," he said.

In an unrelated case, police arrested Alexis Buchanan Harrison, 26, of Tampa, accused of filing tax returns with the names and Social Security numbers of deceased people.[14]

Harrison was charged with two counts of fraudulent use of personal information. She taught others the scheme as well, according to the affidavit for a search warrant executed on her home.

Harrison showed people how to use a genealogy website that lists the names, dates of birth, dates of death, and Social Security numbers for millions of people.

Police confiscated 10 debit cards, $1,100 in cash, jewelry, computers, four TVs, three gaming systems, four cell phones, and gift cards from Harrison's home.

How lucrative are these IRS scams, and how widespread have they become? Two recent cases in Florida supply a vivid answer.

After a joint FBI-Secret Service investigation, a 35-year-old Fort Lauderdale woman was in federal court to answer charges that she and six others filed more than 1,000 false tax returns just since January of 2012.

According to U.S. Attorney Wifredo A. Ferrer, Alci Bonannee was part of a ring that filed a massive number of false returns and had refunds direct deposited into accounts they had set up. According to government documents, Bonannee and her accomplices withdrew approximately $9.5 million from these bank accounts.[15]

When police arrested the woman, a search of her house uncovered a notebook and folder containing more than 1,000 names, dates of birth, and Social Security numbers belonging to identity-theft victims.

Meanwhile, in Tampa, a former Ocala Police Officer, Dana Brown, was by U.S. District Judge Mary S. Scriven, sentenced to six years and five months in federal prison for conspiracy to make false claims, aggravated identity theft, and exceeding authorized access to a protected computer with intent to defraud.[16]

According to court documents, Brown was a patrol officer for the Ocala Police Department. That gave him access to the Florida Highway Safety and Motor Vehicles Driver and Vehicle Information Database (DAVID) from which he could retrieve driver and vehicle information.

Brown is alleged to have been working with Riad Sulaiman, a store owner in Tampa. Sulaiman had fraudulently obtained U.S. Treasury tax refund checks in the names of various individuals. Brown provided the information Sulaiman needed to cash the checks using personal identifying information obtained from DAVID. For this, it was charged, he received a piece of the action.

How big was the operation? Brown was ordered to pay more than $874,000 in restitution to the Internal Revenue Service.

The IRS and the Justice Department are also getting more aggressive in pursuing those filing phony claims for refunds. Earlier this year, the Justice Department's Tax Division and local U.S. Attorneys' offices targeted 105 people in 23 states. In all, 939 criminal charges were included in 69 indictments related to identity theft.

The other letter you don't want to get from the IRS is one asking why you did not include on your return income you earned from the XYZ Corporation who has filed a W-2 or Form 1099 with the IRS. Or you might get a letter asking why you have not included the income earned by your son or daughter. Of course, you have never heard of the XYZ Corporation, let alone worked for them. Your son or daughter is five years old and obviously has never worked for the XYZ Corporation, either. What you have in this situation, probably, is an identity thief has used your name and your Social Security number, or your child's name and Social Security number in applying for a job. This is not uncommon in situations where the worker is an undocumented alien who does not have the proper visa or clearance to work in this country.

Here is another dismaying story. Benny Watters, at age five, died of a brain tumor in September 2010. But when almost a year later his parents filed their taxes claiming him as a dependent for the final time, their return was rejected because an identity thief already had filed a return, and received a refund, in Benny's name.[17]

"It was almost like somebody had stolen him from us," said his mother, Lisa Watters of Lake Forest, Illinois, who described in an interview how she quickly found the data needed to co-opt her dead son's identity on the Internet. "It's just so easy, and I don't know what purpose it serves."

This information about Benny Watters, and more than 89 million other people, can be found in the very public Social Security Administration's Death Master File. It is data the Agency uses to stop paying benefits and start paying survivor benefits after people die. Updates to the file covering the recently deceased, is a goldmine for identity thieves who quickly file tax returns and obtain refunds before the legitimate returns arrive at the IRS.

The Death Master File dates to 1980, when the Social Security Administration settled a lawsuit filed under the Freedom of Information Act. Michael Astrue, the administration's commissioner, told a congressional subcommittee that his agency doesn't have the authority to stop making the information available unless Congress passes new legislation.[18]

You can even have your identity partially stolen. I have heard of cases where scammers have used a person's addresses and phone numbers to mask their identities without stealing the person's name or Social Security number. Suddenly, when a flood of calls and mail from collectors starts showing up the collector won't buy that the person they're after does not have this phone number or isn't living at this address.

In such a scenario, you don't have many options. You are not a victim of identity theft in the traditional sense. If you go to the police or to the Federal Trade Commission, they can't help you. Your credit report is fine (although this might change), so filing a fraud report with the agencies will get you nowhere. The only answer might be to first file an identity theft report with the U.S. Postal Service. Please go to http://www.bankrupatbirthbook.com and you'll find a link to where you can file and then change your phone number to an unlisted number and give it out judiciously.

MEDICAL ID THEFT

In recent years, medical identity theft has been on the rise. This is the process of assuming another's identity and, often, insurance information, for the purpose of obtaining medical services. Many articles on the subject cite the use of fraudulent identities to obtain drug prescriptions either for resale or for personal use and abuse. Another situation can best be described as identity theft with permission. A friend who is uninsured needs treatment for an injury or an illness, so you "lend" them your insurance card and "identity." That is why doctor's offices and hospitals today generally require a picture ID also.

But ask Anndorie Sachs, and she can tell you medical identity theft can be much stranger.

One day, the Salt Lake City woman received a frantic call from a local hospital claiming the newborn baby she had just taken home tested positive for illegal drugs in its system.[19]

This, of course, was news to her since it had been more than a few years since she had last given birth. It might have been an amusing case of mistaken identity except that investigators from the state's Department of Child and Family Services showed up the next day threatening to remove her four children and calling her an unfit mother.

"As much as I denied it, they just kept insisting that, yes, I was the mother of this child and there was nothing I could say to get out of it," she told a television interviewer. "They questioned my employer and interrogated my children." Shortly thereafter came hospital bills totaling several thousand dollars.

It turned out that a young pregnant woman and alleged drug abuser had stolen Sachs's driver's license, walked into a hospital, had the baby, and left the hospital with the baby. Of course, Ms. Sachs was left to clean up the mess.

Or ask Linda Weaver of Palm Coast, Florida, who one day opened her mailbox to find a bill from a local hospital for the amputation of her right foot. Since she was standing on both feet she realized some mistake had been made.[20]

She walked into the hospital to clear up the problem and learned that an imposter had somehow gotten hold of her Social Security number, her address, and even her insurance ID number. She was able to clear up the matter, but her problems were not over. A year later when she checked into the same hospital for a procedure, it became apparent the phony Linda Weaver's medical history had become mixed with her own. She now worries that in some future illness of medical emergency, she will receive the wrong treatment.

Hopefully this chapter will have given you a better sense of the types of identity theft out there.

CHAPTER FOUR:

FRIENDS, FOES, AND TOTAL STRANGERS

Most of us probably have a mental image of a bad guy—the gun, the evil stare, the gruff look, etc. The image of the bad guy hasn't really changed all that much from the days of the old Wild West. But, obviously, the modern-day bad guy is much different. He—or she—may carry a briefcase and have an advanced degree on the wall.

This is especially true in the world of identity theft. The "bad guy" might not actually be so bad after all. He—or she—might just be a person who is not careful with information we give them. We live in a trusting society, particularly when it comes to people in positions of authority, be it the receptionist at the physician's office, my daughter's coach, her school administrators, etc. You consider these people to be friends but, as we will see, when it comes to identity theft, they may well be foes.

The insurance company statistics reveal that most car accidents happen within a few miles of home. When it comes to identity theft, you might use a similar metaphor. The thief might be a member of the household, or a stranger who is given the personal information needed to steal an identity. Or it might be an every day contact who we don't think twice about.

You probably see yourself as a cautious parent. You probably also see yourself as a nice person. But it's your obligation, and your job as a parent, to safeguard your children and to safeguard what's theirs. In this chapter, I'll make you more aware of exactly who it is that may be seeking to take your children's identities, and why they do it, so you can take steps to help prevent it.

You're probably asking yourself who steals a child's identity? There is not a simple answer to this question. The more cases we examine, the more complicated this question becomes. To start, we will look at what some of the recent studies have said and that is in a high percentage of identity theft cases, the theft is either familial or its "organized crime."

FRIENDLY FRAUD

As I mentioned in Chapter One, familial or "friendly fraud" as it is sometimes called, is exactly what the term implies. In a surprising number of cases, a young person will discover when turned down for an apartment, or applying for a first car loan or for financial aid that he or she has a spotty credit history because a relative, —often a parent or older sibling or another member of the victim's "household" has used their identity, possibly for years, usually in situations where the relative's own credit has been bad or non-existent.

This represents an all-too typical case. Lt. Mike Rompa of the Bolingbrook, Illinois police said a 48-year old woman came into the police station in June 2011 after receiving overdue notices from several different creditors for accounts she did not open. The accounts included ones for cell phones, utilities, and a BMW.

Eventually, police were able to trace the accounts to the woman's niece, Latonyia N. Brown, who apparently had been using her aunt's identity and good credit for more than a year. "The investigation revealed she had opened up several utility accounts, three cell phones, and purchased a 2004 BMW X5 from a dealership in Bolingbrook with the false identity," Rompa said.[1]

Detectives met with dealership employees to confirm Brown was the person who had actually purchased the car and learned she was expected to have the vehicle serviced at the dealership. Police were waiting and took her into custody where they discovered that she was carrying identification in both her and her aunt's name.

The vehicle was turned over to the dealership.

Other cases of identity theft by family members can be quite sad, as is this one reported by Steven Reilly in the New Jersey Herald: Rachel Mongiovi had been abroad for a year studying and stepped into what she describes as a nightmare that still haunts her years later.

It seems her sisters, Sarah Conklin and Jessica Mongiovi were stopped by Stanhope police on a serious traffic violation. The sisters then stole Rachel's identity, hoping to avoid the repercussions.[2]

In the driving incident, Jessica Mongiovi, the driver, used Rachel's name, birth date, and Social Security number to avoid charges for driving on a suspended license. Police records show that Jessica, aka Rachel, was let go with a traffic ticket. Conklin, however, was arrested on outstanding warrants and taken to the Sussex County Jail.

When Joseph Mongiovi, the father of the sisters, discovered what had happened, he went to the police and said it could not have been Rachel because she was out of the country. Police agreed and tried to expunge the record, but then came another twist in the story.

Jessica and Sarah were arrested and ultimately convicted of giving false information to police. But the prosecutor's office listed Rachel's name, birth date, and Social Security number as Sarah's alias. What this meant was that, while all the charges against Rachel were dismissed, her name was contained in the original complaint that was filed.

When Rachel returned from out of the country, she found her name, birth date, and Social Security number listed as an alias to Conklin's criminal record, which reportedly includes arrests for multiple felonies.

"It is like I don't even exist," Mongiovi told the newspaper. "I have no civil rights to protect me from this. I spent my whole life doing the right thing and working hard, and now I have a criminal record whenever I go for a job."

"I went to Lowe's, where I worked before I went away to college, to try to get one of the five jobs they had advertised, but I was told they had all been filled," Mongiovi said. "I even applied to work as a sales clerk at Dale's Jewelry in the mall, but they made me take an honesty quiz after my record came up, and I still didn't get the job."

"I have been devastated by this. I can't find work in any of the fields I went to school for because of the background check," Mongiovi said. "I have lost my car. I am behind in my loan payments, and I have to move back with my family."

After five years of pleading, all she got from the prosecutor's office is a letter stating:

> "Rachel Mongiovi was considered by this office to be the innocent victim of crimes committed by her sisters. She was not a party to the crimes committed nor did she have any prior criminal history."

Rachel's dream job is to become a civilian administrator at the Picatinny Arsenal. That takes a high level security clearance. Even with the letter, that now seems out of the question.

Javelin Research estimated that in 2011, one out of seven cases of identity theft involved a relative, roommate, coworker, or some other acquaintance of the victim. The average amount stolen in a friendly fraud case, according to Javelin, was $8,233, compared with $3,666 when the scammer is not known to the victim and, moreover, the out-of-pocket cost to the victim is nearly four times higher than in other cases.[3]

Lexington (KY) police detective Wayne Thornton puts this into perspective. He investigates financial crimes that are reported to the Lexington Police and that includes many cases of identity theft. He recently told the Lexington Herald-Leader that perhaps 70 percent of the cases he gets involve someone who stole the identity of a "friend, coworker, or family member."

"The overwhelming majority of my cases are very mundane, small dollar amount cases," said Thornton. "It's typically a brother, a sister, a cousin, father or son, and they want to get cable or utilities such as water and electricity, as well as necessities such as cars and home repairs." In one recent case, he told the newspaper, a Lexington woman allegedly used her sister's identifiers to buy new doors for her home on credit, skipping out on the bill with about $3,000 left to pay.

These cases at times can be heartbreaking. Often the relative has poor credit and vows to do better "starting over" with the child's credit. Sometimes they do, often they do not. Other times, usually in the situation of a broken family, the story is much darker and stark, and the case ends up in court, or even in criminal proceedings. But in either case, you have a young person who finds themselves in a deep hole just starting out.

Here are a couple examples:

Annie (as we shall call her), was a single mom with a son whose birth father was not very engaged with him growing up. So she was a little suspicious when he was 15, and his dad finally took an interest in the young man and bought him his first car. But his dad agreed to take care of registering the car and paying for the car insurance. For more than a year, everything seemed fine. Then Annie's son received a letter from the DMV notifying him that because he was under 18 and had no car insurance he would lose his license until he was 21. His dad had moved out of state and they had no way to reach him. When Annie called the DMV she learned his dad hadn't just registered the car he bought for Annie's son, he had also registered his cars in the boy's name—and then let the car insurance lapse. Her ex, an alcoholic, had lost his license because of multiple DWIs, so he had registered his cars in his son's name so that he could get insurance. It was a mess and took months to straighten everything out and, as a result Annie's son had to sell his car and wait a year before he could buy another car and get insurance.

A starker case is represented by Rebecca Jean Ferguson, a former Berkeley County (West Virginia) public school teacher who found herself in court pleading guilty to eight counts of identity theft as she entered what is known as an Alford plea, in which she did not admit guilt but agreed the state had ample evidence to find her guilty in a trial.[4]

Ferguson admitted to establishing eight credit card accounts using her then 14-year-old daughter's name. The eight accounts were opened in 2005 when the victim was between the ages of 14 and 15, police said. Ferguson couldn't pay back the credit card debts, resulting in her daughter's credit rating being severely impacted.

To complicate matters, Ferguson faced a series of child abuse charges, which she claimed were false and motivated by "revenge."

> "I didn't do it to be mean," she said in a written statement given police. "I did it so we could pay our bills."

I have heard of situations where a police officer has shown up at someone's door to serve a warrant for various driving offenses. Mom has brought out the seven year old named in the warrant and demanded the officer explain how the child could have amassed several years' of unpaid tickets or ignored demands for court appearances. The answer is inevitably the boy's father or uncle or older brother has used the child's identity to obtain a drivers license after theirs was suspended or revoked. This situation occurs so often that police are no longer all that surprised to learn that the person named in the warrant they are serving is barely out of kindergarten.

Familial identity theft adds a whole unpleasant layer to the problem of identity theft. Often, the result is a complete disintegration of family trust and, all too often, the young person is left on their own to try to straighten out the problems. I have heard of situations where the victim eventually simply pays off the debt to clear up their credit report. But, other times, their they turn the matter over to police.

ORGANIZED CRIME

When talking about "organized crime" in the context of child identity theft, by and large we are not talking about organized crime as depicted in The Godfather—the "I'll make him an offer he can't refuse" context. However, such scenarios are not completely unheard of, especially when dealing with some of the eastern European crime gangs who have landed on our shores. Organized crime in the context of identity theft usually refers to a group of persons who steal identities and either: 1) sell, them on the thriving black market for stolen identities—a black market where a stolen child's identity brings top dollar—or 2) use the stolen identities themselves to steal money and goods.

Take for instance Jung-Sook Ko, aka "Grace Lim," of Ridgefield, New Jersey, who was recently sentenced to 41 months in federal prison in a Newark courtroom right down the road from where Tony Soprano captivated audiences for so many years.[5]

According to court documents Ko was arrested in September 2010 as one of 53 individuals in connection with sophisticated identity theft ring and was charged, along with 43 other individuals, with participating in a criminal enterprise allegedly headed by one Sang-Hyun Park. According to prosecutors the gang "obtained, brokered, and sold identity documents to customers for the purpose of committing credit card fraud, bank fraud, and tax fraud."

These kinds of organized groups are becoming all too common. Using very sophisticated means they often hack into databases and steal hundreds, thousands, or even tens of thousands of identities, package them, and then sell them to individuals who use them to commit fraud.

Recently, as part of what they have dubbed "Operation Open Market," the U.S. Secret Service, and Immigration and Customs Enforcement have arrested 19 people—two in Las Vegas and another 17 in California, Florida, New York, Georgia, Michigan, Ohio, New Jersey, and West Virginia—for operating a crime ring that specialized in identity theft and counterfeit credit card trafficking.[6]

This was a very sophisticated criminal organization. In announcing the arrest of the 19, the Secret Service said:

"The defendants are alleged to be members and associates of a criminal organization who traffic in and manufacture stolen and counterfeit identification documents and access device cards (debit and credit cards), and engage in identity theft and financial fraud crimes. The organization encourages members to sell contraband, such as counterfeit documents and stolen bank account information by way of the organization's websites. Higher-level members of the organization examined and tested the products that other members wished to advertise and sell on its websites, and posted summaries of these reviews.

Members of the organization used various procedures to mask their identities from law enforcement and to prevent detection from rival criminal organizations. Contraband available for purchase included money laundering services, fraudulent identification documents, stolen credit card account information, or "dumps," stolen PayPal accounts, and counterfeit plastic and counterfeit holograms used for producing counterfeit credit cards."

This situation is actually worse than first reported. In its initial report to the public, they had arrested 19 named individuals. Actually, 50 people were charged in the investigation but, at the time of the announcement, 39 of those are named defendants and 11 more were only identified as "John Doe" because they always have used aliases.

Investigators have not been able to come to any final numbers on how much was stolen and from whom. But U.S. Attorney Daniel Bogden said, "the extent of the theft and sale of personal information uncovered by this investigation is astonishing."

What should be chilling is that this Las Vegas-based gang is only one of many currently operating in the United States. Finding them and shutting them down has become a top priority of the Secret Service, FBI, and the Justice Department. These are not instances of criminals who are doing things that do not touch us. This should be personal to you because this Las Vegas group and the many others that we know are out to steal your children's identities and ours. They are not going into banks with guns, or hijacking trucks, or running illegal gambling or prostitution rings. The currencies on which their multi-million dollar rings are based are from illicitly obtained identity information. What's even worse is that many of them target children like yours and mine.

OPPORTUNISTIC IDENTITY THEFT

If organized crime is at one end of the spectrum, the other end involves the opportunistic identity thief. Here, the perpetrator is neither a family member nor some organized gang, but rather it is a person or persons who happens to be in the path of the victim's personal information.

A few examples: (Ms.) Danell Adams worked in the financial department of the Greenville (South Carolina) Hospital System. She was arrested on two counts of identity fraud that occurred between April 2011 and March 2012. Police said she had access to patient records and targeted the victims because they had the same last name, Adams, as she did.[7]

She is accused of using information from the victims' personal information to lease an apartment and open accounts with Charter Communications (cable TV) and Duke Energy (Power Company).

Eventually, the Duke and Charter accounts went to collection with a balance of $1,023 total. Adams was found out when one of her victims went away to college and tried to open a credit card account but was denied because of the delinquent accounts.

Then the second victim, who was not a patient at the hospital but rather whose husband worked there, came forward when she received a collection letter trying to collect unpaid rent for Danell Adams' apartment.

The Greenville Sheriff's Office then wisely advised anyone who was or had been a patient or who worked at the Greenville Hospital System, whose last name is Adams, to review their credit reports.

Danell Adams' crime is small potatoes but is an excellent example of identity theft where the victims are simply victims of opportunity. Other crimes of opportunity are not minor.

Melinda Clayton of Montgomery, Ala. worked for Electronic Data Systems Inc. (EDS), for decades one of the nation's largest data-processing firms. In the course of her employment, she had access to countless people's personal and financial data. According to court records, in April of 2011, Clayton was arrested on a criminal complaint following the execution of a search warrant at her house charged in a 43-count superseding indictment with conspiring to defraud the United States by filing false claims, filing false claims, wire fraud, and aggravated identity theft. Various others were also charged with similar crimes.

The search of Clayton's house uncovered tens of thousands of stolen names and Social Security numbers that came from numerous sources, including private companies, health clinics, and prisons, all via EDS.

According to records, the indictment and plea agreement, Clayton and co-conspirators used the stolen identities to file false tax returns and claimed fraudulent tax refunds that they directed the IRS to deposit into bank accounts they set up or to prepaid debit cards they bought. Court documents say they filed at least 155 fraudulent tax returns using stolen identities and sought at least $494,242 in tax refunds. At least 250 persons are known to have had their identities stolen by Clayton.

She was sentenced to 61 months in prison, following a guilty plea to conspiracy to make false claims, wire fraud, and aggravated identity theft. United States District Judge Mark Fuller also ordered her to pay $494,424 in restitution.

Another example of an accidental victim is the story of Stacey Lanius. When she was a student at the University of Texas, still with her maiden name of Stacey Rogers, a student organization she was a member of ran a fundraising event that involved students applying for five credit cards, including a Mastercard and four store cards. The catch was simple. Each credit application resulted in a donation to the organization.[8]

After getting her parents' permission, with the usual warning not to go crazy charging things, Stacy filled out the five applications and turned them in. She never heard back from any of the five, and she assumed that her applications had been declined because she had no credit history. She thought no more of it.

Let's pick up on Stacy's story as she related it to a hearing of the U.S. House of Representatives Ways and Means Social Security Subcommittee. She says:

"Two years later, I made a purchase in Dillards and tried to pay by check. The clerk denied my check and told me that I had to go to customer service. At customer service, I was told that I had exceeded my limit on my Dillards' credit card and was behind on my payments. I told the clerk that I did not have a Dillards' credit card and asked to see the transactions on this account.

"There were numerous transactions on the account spanning two years. I was able to obtain copies of the receipts for the purchases and on one of the receipts was a driver's license number.

"My father (an FBI agent) ran the license number for me, and we discovered that a woman who shared my name, Stacey Rogers, had made the purchases. I drove to the credit bureaus and requested a copy of my credit report. This woman had somehow intercepted the five credit card applications for which I had applied two years before. She changed the address on the accounts so that when the cards were issued, they went straight to her. I never knew I had been approved for the cards. Our best guess at the time was that she worked at the business that processed the applications, saw that we shared a name, and altered the applications. She also kept my Social Security number for future use.

"On my credit report, those five accounts were charged to the max and were delinquent. Additionally, she had used my Social Security number to apply for more credit and financing. There were thousands of dollars in charges and numerous delinquent accounts on my credit history due to this theft of my identity."

Here is a perfect example of identity theft by happenstance. Stacey shared a name with someone who she did not know and whose path she crossed almost by accident. But accident or not, the consequences were very real.

Stacey's poor credit history followed her for years—when she tried getting her first apartment, or her first car, or applying for a credit card. The other Stacey Rogers continued to use her Social Security number to finance everything from televisions to surgeries. Each time she would go to a vendor to explain the problem, or go to the credit bureaus to get the fraudulent purchases off her credit report, she was told that she needed to prove that she had not made the purchases. How does one go about proving a negative?

Stacey diligently visited every credit bureau, circling the accounts that she claimed were fraudulent. The accounts stayed on here record, but a note was added that there was a claim of fraud on the account. In 1991, she married and her legal name changed. Several years later, she finally noticed a decrease in the fraudulent activity.

She now has an excellent credit rating, has successfully financed the purchase of two homes, and is free of the effects of the identity theft. However, the stress the theft caused was tremendous; occurring at a point in her life when she was just getting started as an adult. She now guards her Social Security number very carefully and checks her credit on an annual basis.

These are all examples of victims who are going to be saddled with trying to restore their credit ratings. It can take months or even years to straighten out their tax records with the IRS. They did nothing wrong. They were not careless. But, they were still victims. This story illustrates the importance of how easily identity theft can occur through no fault of the victim. It also points out how it's wise for parents to be proactive in terms of monitoring your child's personal information. Obviously there is a very sharp distinction between people who steal an identity from files they have access to, and the big time organized identity theft gangs like the Las Vegas crew. One of the main things that differentiates the two is the opportunistic thief usually steals one or a few files at a time while the gangs want to steal identities in as large a batch as possible.

FACTS AND FIGURES

Now, I'll give you some almost totally unbelievable figures from last year as compiled by the researchers at the Identity Theft Resource Center (ITRC).

According to the ITRC's 2011 Breach Report last year, 22,521,747 million records (records can mean Social Security numbers, credit cards, financial account numbers, or other pieces of information such as driver's license numbers or medical insurance numbers) were stolen in publicly acknowledged computer break-ins. Malicious attacks (defined by the ITRC as a combination of hacking and insider theft) accounted for nearly 40 percent of the recorded breaches. Of the breaches reported, 61.6 percent involved exposure of Social Security numbers, representing 80.7 percent of known records.

These numbers of records were stolen in some 419 publicly acknowledged breaches, and no one really knows how many more breaches have gone unreported because holders of the data just hope the whole thing will blow over until forced to acknowledge it once malicious uses of the data begin showing up.

I SPOKE EARLIER OF THE BREACH STUDY DONE BY THE VERIZON RISK TEAM IN COOPERATION WITH THE U.S. SECRET SERVICE. A CLOSER LOOK AT THESE BREACHES REVEALED THAT:

» 83% of victims were targets of opportunistic thieves

» 92% of attacks were not very difficult to commit

» 76% of all data was compromised from an organization's servers

» 86% were discovered by a third party, e.g. credit bureau

» 96% were avoidable through simple or intermediate controls, e.g. identity monitoring

KEY FACTS ABOUT BREACHES INVESTIGATED BY VERIZON OR THE U.S. SECRET SERVICE

» 50% of breaches utilized some form of hacking

» 49% used some type of malware

- » 29% were physical attacks, e.g. stolen files

- » 17% came about because of system privilege misuse

- » 11% were the result of the misuse of social media tactics

OTHER SECURITY BREACHES

It's worth thinking about this for a moment. If, for example, you are interested in obtaining batches of children's Social Security numbers, where is the first place you might look? Perhaps you'd go to a place not known for the security it maintains on its computer system and computer records—yes, indeed, your local school system.

John Webb, an Assistant U.S. Attorney based in Nashville, is a recognized expert in financial crimes and ID theft. He sums it up nicely: "Security breaches have become commonplace as more people have access to databases. There are so many ways it can happen. When there is a computer and multiple individuals have access to databases or thumb drives, and there are hackers and stolen laptops, networks are susceptible to breaches."

A major reason children's identities are stolen is to obtain "clean" Social Security numbers that are then used to gain employment. Testimony at a recent U.S. House of Representatives hearing put the percent of undocumented workers who are able to gain employment using stolen Social Security numbers at 75 percent.

AT THAT HEARING VARIOUS EXAMPLES WERE PROVIDED:

- » A 9-year-old boy who was denied Medicaid because wages were reported on his Social Security number.

- » A 13-year-old girl who was denied as a dependent on her family's tax return because she supposedly made too much money.

- » An 11-year-old girl and a 13-year-old girl whose Social Security numbers are being used by multiple people for work authorization.

Jennifer Andrushko testified about her three-year-old son who was a victim. When Andrushko's son was born, the Social Security Administration issued him a Social Security number. Unfortunately, that Social Security number had already been in use for years by an undocumented worker who used it to fraudulently obtain a work permit and to run up unpaid medical bills. Andrushko's son's credit, medical history, work history, and his potential for future Social Security benefits were immediately corrupted.[9]

"In November 2009, my husband found himself unemployed in a falling economy. On Monday, November 16, 2009, I went to the Utah Department of Work Force Services (DWS) to apply for food stamps and Medicaid to help our family get by until my husband was able to gain new employment a month later. During our eligibility interview over the phone, the eligibility specialist informed me that wages were being reported to my then 3-year-old son's Social Security number since 2007. I inquired as to where the wages were being reported and to whom, and was told that, due to the Privacy Act, I was not allowed to have that information, although they had it. Later, it was brought to my attention that we could have been denied aid because my son was 'earning too much money.'"

"I cannot express how ridiculous it is that my son's Social Security number has been used for care at an OB/GYN's office or how frightening it is to know that my son's medical history has been blatantly corrupted, which could have a serious impact on my son's life and medical care," Andrushko said in her testimony.

Often, the immigrants who use these stolen numbers are themselves victims of unscrupulous lawyers or "consultants" who sell them so-called "Credit Protection Numbers." Such numbers, which they are told to use until the day they get legitimate documentation, are frequently stolen Social Security numbers of children.

In a very sad case in 1982, three-year-old Jason Evers died during a Cincinnati kidnapping. In 1996, Doitchin Krastev, a Bulgarian immigrant, apparently learned of the decade-old crime and applied to the Cincinnati records office for a copy of the birth certificate of Jason Robert Evers. Upon receiving it,

Krastev applied for, and obtained, a Social Security number in the name of Jason Robert Evers. In 2002, he used the identity to apply for a U.S. Passport, which he received.[10]

Over the next 14 years, Krastev/Evers lived in Bend, Oregon, and had a very successful career working for the State of Oregon's Liquor Control Commission. In 2008, he was promoted to regional manager and the OLCC moved him to Medford.

Last year, he applied to get his passport renewed in Boise, Idaho, and that was his undoing. Krastev's identity theft was uncovered as part of "Operation Death Match," a United States Diplomatic Security Service program that now routinely compares passport applications to state death certificates. He was immediately arrested.

Charged with aggravated identity theft and passport fraud, Krastev would not reveal his true identity. But, now, as part of a plea bargain, he has identified himself, and agreed to meet with Jason Robert Evers' family members to apologize and to answer their questions.

He's faces 24 months in prison and then deportation.

Mr. Krastev's story illustrates a couple of important points. Using the Social Security number of a deceased child, how was he able to secure employment with a state agency? That is a question being asked in Oregon, because the OLCC is supposed to be an agency that checks and double checks the credentials of perspective employees.

But along these same lines, there exists a system called E-Verify. U.S. law requires companies to employ only individuals who may legally work in the United States—either U.S. citizens or foreign citizens who have the necessary authorization. The U.S. Department of Homeland Security maintains the system, in cooperation with the Social Security Administration which—as the name would indicate—verifies that a perspective employee possesses the necessary authorization to be legally employed. The problem is that the use of the law is voluntary except in a limited number of states where it is required of some employers, but only a few that requires its use by all employers. For years, attempts to mandate its use nationally has failed in Congress, opposed by small business organizations, agricultural groups, and others who claim it is too difficult or time consuming to use.

If its use were mandated, and if the penalties for hiring an illegal worker, absent an E-Verify clearance, were strengthened, then the theft of children's identities to be used to gain employment would be reduced or even eliminated.

Mr. Krastev's story also illustrates the fact that child identity theft left undetected, can drag on for a very long time. In this case, it was the sad fact that the victim was deceased. But had Jason Evers simply been three when his identity was stolen, he would have just about been at the age where he was applying for college or a driver's license or a first job and suddenly would have found half a continent away he had been living and working and developing a credit history.

Children are prime targets of this kind of identity theft. It is highest in the states with the largest populations of undocumented workers. In Utah, the state found that 1,626 companies were paying wages to the Social Security numbers of children on public assistance under the age of 13.

In our next chapter, we'll examine the vulnerability of your children's Social Security numbers. By understanding where and how your kid's SSNs are most vulnerable, you'll be able to do more to protect them. Think of it like getting a lock on the front door of your child's identity. It won't prevent every crime, but it can make them a less appealing target for thieves.

See where you can reduce risk for your kids.
Visit **www.BankruptAtBirthBook.com**
to download your own
Risk Factors Checklist.

CHAPTER FIVE:

OUR CHILD'S MOST VALUABLE POSSESSION

Why do people steal children's identities? Why do they want to steal your child's? What does your child have they most want?

The answer is simple—a child's Social Security number to the identity thief is the Holy Grail.

My wife is usually the one who takes my daughters to the doctor or dentist. As you might expect, when she checks in, she is often asked for the kids' Social Security numbers. In return, she politely asks a very simple question, "Why do you need that information?" Very often the response is something like—we just need a unique number, you can use a phone number if you prefer.

Your children's identities shouldn't be exposed. You will find there's rarely a good reason for someone needing their SSN. When my wife is asked for either of our children's Social Security numbers, she just declines. Nothing negative has resulted.

This chapter will ask another question you may never have considered: Why does your child need to know their Social Security number? You will see not only that they don't, but that it's best you don't tell them until they absolutely need to know it.

This chapter will show the evolution of the Social Security number and how we have gotten to the never-intended point it has become a kind of national identifier. It is a complicated evolution.

Any discussion of how to protect your children from identity theft, how we protect our kids, is necessarily a three-prong discussion. The first prong involves your child's Social Security number—when and where you should give that number out, how you can determine whether your information will be protected, and how you can, as a parent, influence its need, its use, and its safety.

The second prong involves protecting your child from inadvertently exposing his or her vital information through their use of social media. This becomes more and more critical every day and is an area that is continually evolving. We will discuss this in Chapter Six.

The third prong is how to first establish that your child's identity has not already been stolen or compromised, so as to establish a baseline. Once this is established, we'll look at how to set up a system and to continually monitor their identity so as to reduce the risk of it being compromised in the future. We will discuss this more in Chapter Eight.

USE OF YOUR CHILD'S SOCIAL SECURITY NUMBER

If life were simple, we could sum up this section in just three words: Just Say No! Say no if you are asked to supply your child's Social Security number. But as we all know, life is far from simple, and so is the use of your child's Social Security number.

Actually, the place to start this discussion of your child's Social Security number is with a simple common-sense rule: Don't tell your children their Social Security numbers! If they don't know it, they can't innocently list it somewhere on an application or online. Perhaps, as they reach their teen years, there might be a need for them to know it but, hopefully, by that time they will understand the danger of listing it somewhere and will think twice before doing it. In the meantime, tell your kids to bring home any kind of document that asks them for their Social Security number for your review.

Now, think back. How many times have you been handed a clipboard and asked to give your child's Social Security number? What were the circumstances? Did the request seem reasonable? Doctor? Dentist? Scout Troop? Insurance applications? Emergency-room visits? Sports teams? Of course, you probably have been asked by their schools. (This is the most complicated issue, so we'll save this discussion for the moment.) You most likely never gave the request a second thought and simply listed the number on the application or in the required column.

Recently, we talked with a group of mothers about identity theft, and several expressed the idea that they are more comfortable giving their children's Social Security numbers at their pediatrician's or dentist's offices because, well, they are trusted people. That's understandable, but these practitioners are trusted to cure illness and toothaches, not have hack-proof computer systems or employees who must first go through intensive security screening and background checks. Also, most medical practices store their electronic records, and paper records, with outside vendors. How safe is the data there?

In a rather startling recent survey, the Michigan based Ponemon Institute found that many small healthcare organizations and medical practices that responded said they've suffered some sort of data breach in the past year. Ninety-one percent of respondents with 250 employees or less said they had suffered at least one data breach, and 23 percent said they experienced at least one patient medical identity theft in that time span.

Major factors for such breaches included negligent employees and an inability to meet compliance requirements, according to the study's authors. Mobile device use and social media activity were considered to be areas of particular vulnerability.

Based on what we have shared thus far, we think that from this point forward, you'll ask "why?" whenever a person or organization requests your child's Social Security number. The answer may be quite valid: At the doctor's office or at the hospital, they require it because your insurance company requires it. This is because it's how they, the insurance company, identify policy holders and dependents who qualify for coverage.

Conversely, if the answer is that using the Social Security number is how the doctor's office keeps track of patients, members, applicants, or what-have-you, then your next question should be: "Thank you. Now, can you help me understand how exactly you protect these numbers?" If the answer to this question seems reasonable, and if they protect the numbers by encrypting the data and use sophisticated firewalls and anti-virus protection to keep out hackers, then maybe you will be inclined to share the number. Otherwise, politely decline, and if necessary, escalate the conversation until you reach the decision maker of the organization.

Most likely, you won't be the only parent balking at giving up your child's Social Security number. If you do decline, there will likely be no material consequences.

The good news is that, more and more, we are running into situations in our daily lives where doctors, dentists, and other service providers are no longer asking for Social Security numbers but have begun using other identifiers. Birthdays or telephone numbers are being used, but mostly birthdays because they don't change when you move. Yes, the medical practice may have multiple patients with the same birthday—in fact, they probably do—but first using the birthday, then the name, gets them to the record they want in a couple of key strokes and actually is easier than working with a nine-digit Social Security number.

You may run across the seemingly simple advice: just lie. When you are asked for your child's Social Security number—just make one up. That solution seems to have multiple pitfalls. First, you are going to have to remember that number if you are in a situation where you have to use the number with the same provider in the future, especially in an emergency situation. You could make up a number that's a single digit off from the correct number, and always use it so it will be easy to remember.

That could work if you don't mind breaking any number of laws. But one area where you really could get into trouble is with medical and dental practices. As we noted within the area of identity theft, one of the fastest-growing segments is what is broadly called medical identity theft. So if you give a wrong Social Security number for your child, and that gets into his/her record at some point, an insurance company is going to see the number does not jibe with its records and now you have a problem to unravel.

Moreover, depending on where you gave this altered number, you might succeed in getting a credit file or, more likely, a medical history file established in your child's name with a wrong Social Security number and that could be asking for future problems. Perhaps the Social Security number you made up is actually someone else's number already.

Now let's return to the central question of this chapter: the gathering and use of students' Social Security numbers by schools, school districts, state school systems and the federal government.

The safety of the school's computer system aside, back to the basic question of why does your child's school need his or her Social Security number? If you ask them why, the answer may be "Because we are required to collect by the school district or the state educational system." If you ask the school district the same question, the response likely will be "Because we are required by the state board of education," or whatever your state's highest education administration is called. Ask the question of them, and the inevitable the response will be along the lines of "The federal government (usually the U.S. Department of Education) requires we collect it."

Ask the DOE, and they will tell you that, not only do they not require it; they actively discourage schools from collecting student Social Security numbers and using them as identifiers. But then ask the Social Security Administration, and its experts will tell you that The Department of Education does require student Social Security numbers in certain circumstances, and therefore many states feel they have no choice except to collect the data.

Whew! How do we get to the bottom of this clash? It seems like it comes down to a he-said/she-said kind of argument.

I'll try to sort it all out for you.

Examining the use and collection of student Social Security numbers in schools starts with the Social Security Administration's Inspector General, Patrick P. O'Carroll, Jr. In July 2010, Mr. O'Carroll took an in-depth look at the use of

Social Security numbers by schools, school districts, and state school systems. The practices that he discovered and the laws and regulations they are based upon, are often contradictory and quite confusing.[1]

The Social Security Administration Inspector General was dismayed to discover that millions of children enroll in K-12 schools each year. To assist in this process, K-12 schools may collect and use Social Security numbers for various purposes. Although no single federal law regulates overall use and disclosure of Social Security numbers by K-12 schools, the Privacy Act of 1974, Social Security Act, and Family Educational Rights and Privacy Act of 1974 (FERPA), contain provisions that govern disclosure and use of Social Security numbers.

Additionally, the Office of Management and Budget (OMB) issued a memorandum in 2007 on safeguarding against and responding to disclosure of personally identifiable information, including Social Security numbers. Federal agencies are required to reduce the volume of collected and retained personally identifiable information to the minimum necessary, including establishment and implementation of plans to eliminate unnecessary collection and use of Social Security numbers. We reviewed relevant state laws, policies and practices regarding collection and use of Social Security numbers in K-12. We also contacted selected state educational agencies to identify steps states have taken to limit K-12 schools' collection and use of Social Security numbers.

Despite the increasing threat of identity theft, our review of state laws and school policies and practices disclosed that K-12 schools' collection and use of Social Security numbers was widespread. We determined that many K-12 schools used Social Security numbers as the primary student identifier or for other purposes, even when another identifier would have sufficed.

What the Inspector General seems to be saying is that no federal law or regulation affirmatively requires schools to collect students' Social Security numbers, but then no federal law or regulation forbids them from doing so either. If this information is gathered, federal regulations require that it must be safeguarded, and the dissemination of all or part of a student's record is regulated by various privacy laws. But, of course, there are no specific requirements for the degree of safeguarding.

In its research, the Inspector General's office identified seven states—Alabama, Arkansas, Florida, Georgia, Kentucky, Virginia, and West Virginia—that, by law, require K-12 schools to obtain students' Social Security numbers. Our company is in Virginia, so this state requirement is extremely troubling and extremely personal for us. The researchers also found that 26 other states—Connecticut, Delaware, Hawaii, Illinois, Iowa, Kansas, Louisiana, Maine, Maryland, Massachusetts, Michigan, Mississippi, Missouri, Nebraska, Nevada, New Hampshire, Ohio, Oklahoma, Oregon, Pennsylvania, Rhode Island, South Carolina, Texas, Utah, Wisconsin, and Wyoming collect students' Social Security numbers even though no specific law in those states require them to do so.

Now, back to Inspector General O'Carroll. There has been a growing trend among State Departments of Education to establish longitudinal databases, which may include Social Security numbers, of K-12 children in a state to track students' progress over time. While some state laws may require that K-12 schools collect Social Security numbers in some instances, we believe some do so as a matter of convenience—because Social Security numbers are unique identifiers and most students have a Social Security number. However, we do not believe administrative convenience should ever be more important than safeguarding children's personal information.

We believe the unnecessary collection and use of Social Security numbers is a significant vulnerability for this young population.

Recent data indicate the number of children under age 19 whose identities have been stolen is growing. This is particularly troubling given that some of these students may not become aware of such activity until they apply for a credit card or student loan. Because of the numerous incidences of identity theft and the recognition that Social Security numbers are linked to vast amounts of personal information, some states have taken steps to limit the collection and use of Social Security numbers. We are encouraged by these efforts and believe that state and local educational systems should seek additional ways to limit their collection and use of Social Security numbers and implement stringent controls to protect Social Security numbers when collected.

Here is where things begin to get even more complicated. The Inspector General also alluded to a growing trend: the establishment of statewide massive databases of all K-12 students in order for the Department of Education to track their progress over time—in some cases even after they graduate and move onto post-secondary schools or into the workforce. While the Department of Education does not instruct states to collect Social Security numbers when establishing longitudinal databases, at least 28 states do so out of convenience.

The U.S. Department of Education has a program called the Statewide Longitudinal Data Systems Grant Program. The department says this grant program is "designed to aid state education agencies in developing and implementing longitudinal data systems to enhance the ability of states to efficiently and accurately manage, analyze, and use education data, including individual student records."

Many states will tell you the Departments of Education requires the use of Social Security numbers. No, says the Department of Education: it says that it only requires students be given unique identifiers, but it does not forbid the use of Social Security numbers.

But this longitudinal database issue gets even murkier when you begin to talk about trying to follow students into their post-secondary lives. There are federal laws and regulations that do require student Social Security numbers at the college level to track federal financial aid recipients, to identify students who take part in or receive benefits from federally funded programs, or who are being tracked in certain databases measuring post-secondary attainment. Many of these regulations deal with federal higher education funding programs, federal guarantees of student loans, federal grants, and the like. Since colleges require Social Security numbers as identifiers, on the state level it is certainly easier and thus more tempting and to track students into their college lives.

Or at least, that's what they say.

So the Inspector General's investigators found that 33 states are collecting student Social Security numbers. To be fair, some of these states also assign separate unique identifiers to every student, and basically use their own systems of unique identifiers in day-to-day use and for research and data collection. But they also do collect and do keep a student's record —the Social Security number.

Most troubling, the Inspector General's investigators found a very wide degree of protection given to these databases and student records. Some states encrypt the data, while some don't. Some store the records deep in cyber-theft-hardened computer systems, while some seem to have very vulnerable systems. Some even outsource the record storage, and some of those contracts do not speak to any level of security the contractor must maintain.

We're sure that when you question your local school or school district's request for your child's Social Security number, you will undoubtedly be reassured by school authorities that your child's data will be protected and safeguarded by the school in its modern computer system. The people giving you these reassurances are probably very sincere. But, despite all these heartfelt assurances, let's take a look at a few recent incidents.

In Fairfax County, where we live and work, the online education system used by the Fairfax County public schools was recently breached. The culprit used the county system to change teachers' and staff members' passwords, change or delete course content, and change course enrollment data. But the culprit didn't cover his tracks very well, and police obtained a search warrant for the home of the woman suspected of being the hacker. She was questioned, and it quickly became clear her depth of computer abilities fell far short of what she would have needed to accomplish this cyber attack. Instead, the guilty party was her nine-year-old fourth-grade son whose name police withheld because he was a minor.

"He's a very intelligent nine-year-old," McLean Officer Don Gotthardt said, "with no criminal intent." He was not charged but likely lost his computer privileges for awhile.

Likewise, a pair of students, one a junior and one a senior, successfully hacked into a Birdville, Texas school district network server through the process of trying to guess teacher passwords. It apparently was not too difficult. They had access to 14,500 student names and Social Security numbers. The security breach was discovered and involved a network server that was no longer in use but still tied to the system network. It was immediately taken out of service.[2]

A more serious breach occurred in the administrative computer system of suburban Maryland's Winston Churchill high school. School officials admitted they did not know the identity of the hacker or hackers and that the breach may have been going on for more than a year. The hackers gained access by using a keylogger on a school computer to capture passwords. (A keylogger is a type of software that captures [or "logs"] keystrokes on a keyboard.) Grade changing was the apparent motive. Teachers at the 2,100-student school were asked to review their grades for several years for discrepancies and to immediately change their system access passwords.[3]

In his report, Inspector General O'Carroll kept coming back to how dangerous the collection and storage of Social Security numbers is by schools and school systems. He included a short list of known break-ins to school and educational system computer systems done for the specific purpose of stealing the identities of students.

The most notorious case occurred in 2009, when it was discovered that some 12,000 Puerto Rican students, teachers, and school administrators had been victims of identity theft by a gang that stole their information and then sold it to undocumented immigrants. The documents were sold as sets (Social Security cards and birth certificates) starting at $150 for originals or $40 copies. A search carried out by the FBI at one of the houses where the gang members lived, led to the discovery of 5,000 identification documents of different types, from birth certificates to Social Security cards.[4]

A side note: Puerto Rico seems to be a major target of child identity thieves because children born there are immediately U.S. citizens and most, have Hispanic names—perfect to sell to undocumented immigrants seeking entry to the U.S. job market.

Thousands of students and district employees of the El Paso Independent School District were put at risk when the district's internal network, which included the names, addresses, and Social Security numbers for approximately 63,000 students and 9,000 employees, was hacked.[5]

EPISD OFFICIALS RELEASED THIS LETTER TO PARENTS:

"Dear Employees, Parents, and Students:

We regret to inform you that the Internal Network (myepisd.org) at the El Paso Independent School District (EPISD) has been infiltrated by an unknown entity (hacked). This infiltration has resulted in the illegal access to teacher and student information by the hacker(s), which is information that includes names, birthdates, addresses, and Social Security numbers.

We are working diligently to identify how this occurred; however, we believe it is imperative that we communicate this information as soon as possible to you so that you are able to take immediate action to protect your personal information and accounts, both current and future.

Please refer immediately to the following websites: http://www.ftc.gov/idtheft or http://www.fightidentitytheft.com. These sites will provide you with the immediate steps you can take to protect your identity, which include fraud alerts and a credit freeze.

We immediately alerted the FBI's Infragard Division to report the breach and will continue to provide you with updated information regarding this situation. We are taking this breach extremely seriously and will continue to take all possible action to address this issue."

In this case, the school district may have caught a break in that the hackers apparently did not have a nefarious intent. The hackers, using the name "Host Bustorz," claimed on a website they broke into the district's network but indicated they would not post Social Security numbers online.

The hackers claimed to have downloaded 49 databases with titles such as athletics, training, and nurse evaluations. As proof, they posted a short list of students' names, ethnicity, and student identification numbers. They said they downloaded students' Social Security numbers but would not post them. They were not encrypted but in plain text the hacker said, then added, "I'll not disclose any of that though."

Actually, it turned out the posting on the Host Bustorz website was the initial tip-off that the school district's system had been hacked. A chief privacy officer for a computer security company in New York noticed the new website and notified El Paso school-district officials that their system had been hacked.

Sometimes hacking into school computer systems is not even necessary because the schools and school systems themselves make stealing identities so very easy. Take, for example, in December 2009 when a North Carolina school system accidentally sent out about 5,000 postcards with students' Social Security numbers (which they had collected as primary student identifier) printed on the front.[6]

Then, in November 2009, documents with students' Social Security numbers visible on each, from a Texas school district's lunch program for 2003 to 2006 were left at a television news station with a note attached claiming the documents were found at a recycling center.[7]

Then there were some 18,541 Metro Nashville students whose Social Security numbers and other data were left exposed online for three months by a consultant's error. Boston-based Public Consulting Group Inc. holds a contract with the state of Tennessee to collect student data from various districts in order to prepare an integrated database for the state education department to utilize various ways.[8]

Stephen Skinner, an owner, said the error happened when workers running a test on random student data inadvertently stored a file to an insecure directory. The files contained student names, gender, race or ethnicity, date of birth, Social Security number and, in some cases, parent names.

How the error was found is interesting. A parent Googled her daughter's name, just out of curiosity, and found a listing for her daughter in the publicly accessible database. Coincidently, she actually worked for the Metro Nashville district and realized she should not have been able to access this information on her daughter on a publicly available database. She immediately passed what she saw up the chain, and when the contractor was called he rightly panicked and immediately took down the database.

"I want to reinforce our deep regret for putting the city of Nashville, the Department of Education and the families of Nashville in this situation where they're going to have to be worried about their identity being out there," Skinner said. "We hope our offer (of one year of credit monitoring) is taken full advantage of by all the families so the burden will be minimized."

Letters were sent out from the school district to the parents acknowledging the error and suggesting that credit reports be monitored just in case.

More recently, seniors at Tarpon Springs High School in Florida had their personal information exposed when a guidance counselor inadvertently sent out a mass email that included student Social Security numbers—which were used as student identifiers.[9]

The guidance counselor sent the message out to Tarpon's entire senior class of approximately 400 students and parents regarding the Bright Futures Scholarship program. The message included two attachments that listed every senior's name and their student ID number—their Social Security number.

School systems are also very vulnerable to inside jobs, to employees, or others who have access to school-system databases. There are many examples of this, but here are a couple.

In August 2010, it is alleged that Tizrah Ingram-Johnson was working for the school board and opened an account with Florida Power & Light under the name of a student. From her office at the school system, she faxed copies of the student's driver's license to the utility company to open an account. She then ignored months' worth of bills totaling $1,046.[10]

Miami-Dade is used to these problems. In 2009, Roshell Demps—a former clerk for the school board—and her boyfriend pleaded guilty to credit card and identity fraud after she was caught stealing Social Security numbers to obtain credit cards.[11]

Sheyla Diaz, a former high school teacher in neighboring Broward County, was sentenced to six months on house arrest for stealing students' identities. She pleaded guilty to a federal identity theft charge, admitting she filled out credit card applications using the names and other personal information of former high school students

At times it is hard to get details on some thefts of information from schools and school districts. An example, Albany, Georgia police arrested Earnest Lee Williams who was a student at Monroe Comprehensive High School and also worked after school in the school office. He was found with a notebook containing a list of 76 student names with their Social Security numbers, addresses, and dates of birth, parents' names and telephone numbers. He apparently simply copied it all out of student files. Not much information was forthcoming from the school system.[12]

Other times, thieves take a more direct approach. One night, the Faustino Fuentes School on Puerto Rico's eastern coastline was broken into using a baseball bat to break down a door. Did the thieves want computers or office equipment or even the petty-cash box? Nope. Stolen from a locked file cabinet were the birth certificates and other identity documents including Social Security numbers of 105 students.[13]

Finally, the Inspector General's investigators found, while some states have record retention limits and destroy some records after a number of years, others have none and keep the data indefinitely. In doing so, they stretch out the period of venerability of those records indefinitely.

Fortunately, there is light the end of this tunnel. We are at the beginning of a definite trend away from the collection of student Social Security numbers. By law, four states—Nebraska, North Dakota, Washington, and Wyoming—have forbidden such collection by schools and this movement is spreading.

But with all this as background, what do you do if you show up at registration and are required to give your child's Social Security number?

Our best advice is to do what we do—ask questions. Why do they need it? The answer you might get is some form of "the state (or federal government) requires us to." If your child is in the federally financed free school lunch program (authorized under the National School Lunch Act), that may be true, but there is no known federal requirement for a Social Security number. If they say the "state" requires it (if you don't live in one of the seven states listed above that do require Social Security numbers by law), simply ask why. Ask if the state or the school itself doesn't supply its own identifier. If it does, ask why the Social Security number is needed.

We'll supply our children's Social Security numbers if the school is able to show a compelling reason for it. The school's convenience is not a compelling reason. You might want to adopt this approach. What it comes down to is simply asking why, and if the answer you get is not satisfactory, then just say no!

Actually, if you refuse to supply your child's Social Security number, you are on sound legal ground. Section 7(a) of the federal Privacy Act of 1974 addresses the use of Social Security numbers by federal, state, or local governments (including school districts) and states the following: "It shall be unlawful for any federal, state or local government agency to deny to any individual any right, benefit, or privilege provided by law because of such individual's refusal to disclose his Social Security account number."

This section goes on to provide two exceptions to the provision: (1) where the disclosure is required by federal statute, or (2) where disclosure relates to records that pre-date the adoption of the Privacy Act of 1974 (January 1, 1975), if such disclosure was required under statute or regulation adopted prior to such date to verify the identity of an individual.

By way of example, the State of Missouri Board of Education notified schools in its state:

"In summary, it is not a violation for the school district to ask for disclosure of the Social Security number, as requirements of the act are met. In most situations, this would require notice that the disclosure is voluntary, a statement outlining why the number is requested, and a description of how the information is to be used. Since refusal to disclose a Social Security number cannot be grounds for exclusion from a program, then the school district must be prepared to substitute an alternative number as an identifier."

The U.S. Justice Department sums it up this way:[14]

"Some school districts request a student's Social Security number when students enroll in order to use it as a student identification number. A district may request a student's Social Security number, but only if it (1) informs the student and parent that providing it is voluntary and (2) explains for what purpose the number will be used. However, a school district may not prevent your child from enrolling in school if you choose not to provide a Social Security number."

We should note that many state education boards are reminding schools that they cannot deny enrollment to a student who (or whose parents) refuse to divulge the student's Social Security number. As much as we might wish this were true because of some newfound awareness and sensitivity to identity theft, almost universally it is to put the school or school district in sync with the Supreme Court's ruling on the rights of the children of undocumented workers to a public education. Most of these children do not posses Social Security numbers; thus, to require a number as a pre-requisite to enrollment is now essentially illegal. But parents, whose concern is the safeguarding their children's personal data, should not be afraid to take advantage. So again we say: Just say "No!"

Most kids don't know their SSN, so parents are the first line of defense for protecting that information. But there is other personal information which kids do know that a criminal can use to piece together enough information to guess a password to an account that might lead them to the number. It probably won't surprise you that the biggest threat parent's face for that to happen is in social media. So in the next chapter, we'll talk about social media and what your kids need to know.

Visit **www.BankruptAtBirthBook.com**
to download
The Child ID Theft Safety Tele-class
led by Author Joe Mason.

CHAPTER SIX:

IGNITING THE EPIDEMIC

I n this day and age, there are few topics as urgent as safety, security, privacy, and social media. How do we keep ourselves and our children safe? This is a surprisingly complicated question.

When I was a kid growing up, much of our recreation was tied to the outdoors. My dad hunted and fished, and he gave me my first BB gun when I was about six. I know this fact may lead to some eye-rolling, but that's okay. I get it. However, it was with that BB gun that my father taught me how to use and respect a firearm.

I think of the BB gun as a metaphor for computers today. Steve and I have a difference of opinion as to when our children should be exposed to computers, when they should be able to go online, and when they should own technology such as cell phones. There are two schools of thought, and both are valid. Steve believes, and I understand why, that there is no need for a child to have, say, a Facebook page until their teen years and a cell phone not until they are well into their high school years.

When my daughter was about three, I introduced her to Microsoft's "Paint" program on the computer. She spent hours with it. Like my BB gun, she learned about the computer, how to use it, and how to respect it. She quickly went through the "Paint" phase, then on to Webkinz, which is now a distant memory for her, except of course, for the shelves of Webkinz stuffed animals.

So, she grew up with the computer, it was important for me to teach her early on to be safe in this connected world that she—and we—have grown to embrace. Every day, I see what happens to people who aren't safe online. I wanted my kids to respect the computer and the cyber world—it can be fun, entertaining, and practical, but it can also be dangerous.

In this chapter, we'll look at the various phases of childhood and young adulthood and the technologies associated with them, namely social media. We'll discuss what's appropriate for what age group. But as with the rest of this book, we will keep returning to our central theme: How do we keep our children safe?

We have seen how often adults are tricked into unwittingly divulging information about themselves and their financial and credit data to scam artists. Children are just as susceptible to being tricked into doing this, and probably more so. Your pre-schooler probably won't fall for some phishing attempt, nor will your second grader. But as those kids get older and find their way to the Internet, or get their first cell phone, as they begin texting or tweeting and social networking, the dangers and the degree of exposure grows exponentially.

Most parents are simply not equipped to really understand the dangers of social networking. Sure, in the abstract, you as the average parent can see the danger. But how many parents really understand how Facebook, Google+, or other social websites really work or understand what dangers lurk in this new world of texting and tweeting, photo posting, Gmail or Hotmail. Yes, you could just say no and forbid your child from entering this world. That might be a viable answer if your child is perhaps eight or younger. But as you either already know or will find out, the pressure soon grows with age, and by their tween years you will likely have to relent. We'll try to prepare you for the inevitable.

SOCIAL NETWORKING 101

The following is a brief introduction to all the various social networking sites out there today. Unless you're part of the minority, you probably know that Facebook is a website on which users first register for free, and then establish a personal home page and profile. Their profile can include things like hometown, religious or political beliefs, favorite music, etc. and be viewable by anyone who is given access to their profile (their "friends").

Members of Facebook can link to the home pages of others through a process called "friending." They then can exchange messages, see the postings and profiles of others who they have "friended," and can continually update their profiles, postings, and be notified when their "friends" do the same.

Data filed with Facebook's 2012 IPO shows that more than 13 percent of the world's population is now on Facebook. According to a filing with the Securities and Exchange Commission, Facebook says it has 901 million monthly active users—a 33 percent jump from a year earlier. Of these 901 million users, Facebook says 526 million of them (58.3 percent) use the site every day. That's a 41 percent increase in a year. Moreover, says Facebook, 488 million of monthly active users (MAUs) used Facebook's mobile apps in March of 2012.[1]

In the United States, Facebook has 158 million users and, in May of 2012, for the first time since Virginia-based ComScore has been keeping track, that number did not rise from the previous month. The average amount of time visitors spent on the site during the month rose to an average of 381 minutes.[2]

In addition, according to Facebook's own recent statistics only 10 percent of users have less than 10 friends, 20 percent have less than 25 friends, while 50 percent (the median) have over 100 friends. The average friend count is 190, according to Facebook and 245 according to a 2011 study from the Pew Research Center's American Life Project.[3]

Twitter is an online social networking service that enables its registered users to send and receive text posts to and from other users they have linked to (or "followed"). The post have to be quite short, a maximum of 140 characters. These are known as "tweets," and the process of sending such messages is known as "tweeting." Users can also send search queries. Most of these messages originate and are read by cellular phones. Twitter has over 500 million users worldwide and 100 million in the United States, and gains in popularity every day.[4]

Texting is the process of sending or receiving text messages usually between two mobile devices or between computers or computers and mobile devices. These messages can contain pictures, video, or sound files. These messages can be of almost any length, but are usually short particularly when sent from a mobile device. The Nielsen Company analyzed mobile usage data among teens in the United States for the second quarter of 2010 (April 2010–June 2010).[5] Their researchers found that American teens on average send or receive 3,339 texts a month—that's more than six per every hour they're awake. Using data from monthly cell phone bills of more than 60,000 mobile subscribers as well as survey data from over 3,000 teens, they found teen females send and receive an average of 4,050 texts per month. Teen males also outpace other male age groups, sending and receiving an average of 2,539 texts. Young adults (age 18–24) come in a distant second, exchanging 1,630 texts per month—a meager three texts per hour.

Google+ (notice the +). This site and service is different from the google.com you probably use every day to find information. "Plus," as it has come to be called, is a new and rapidly growing social networking site started by Google to try to rival Facebook. It made its first appearance in June of 2011. It is available online via computer or on mobile devices. It integrates social services such as Google Profiles and Google Buzz, and introduces new services identified as "circles," "hangouts," "huddles," and "sparks." Users gather their friends into circles and can see updates that have been posted by those in their circles. In turn, that can input text and post to their circle. They can also share photos and videos with their circles. When Google+ first launched, it was deemed for adults only. But now, after additional privacy safeguards have been added, the minimum age for joining has been lowered to 13.

Pinterest is a photo and video sharing website that allows members to create and manage image and video collections on "pinboards," and invite others to view, all while having them available for all other members to view. It is possible for members to use photos pinned to other boards in their own collections or to comment on them. Pinterest says its mission is nothing short of "connecting everyone in the world through the 'things' they find interesting." It also says it is the fastest-growing social site. This is partially true because it started from zero in 2010. In February 2012, Pinterest had 10.4 million users.[6]

Foursquare, is a location-based social networking website built for mobile devices, primarily smartphones that have GPS capabilities. Since it began in 2009, its popularity has grown among older teens and young adults. Using an app they have downloaded to their phone or other "smart" device, when users arrive at a bar, a restaurant or a venue, they see if the location is contained on their Foursquare app and they tap a key to "check in." Once they do, others with the Foursquare app who they have designated—like friends on Facebook—know where they are, and likewise, they can see where their friends are at any one time if those friends have also checked-in. New additions to the service now allow you to constantly see where your friends are as they move around, and they can also see where you move. Another feature, if you chose, allows friends to see where you have been over the past two weeks. Some bars and restaurants will give discounts or other incentives for checking in.

For privacy sake, the site says nothing about you except where you were at a given point-in-time. But, with its tracking feature, it does allow friends to chart your progression from place to place as you check in.

You certainly can be forgiven if you never heard of Instagram, or at least never heard of it before Facebook paid $1 billion to acquire the 18-month old start-up with 13 employees and no profits. It is another photo sharing site allowing users to adjust and improve photos taken with cell phone camera and then immediately post them for all to see. The site took a couple of programmers just eight weeks to build and it started with 25,000 users in its first months. By February of 2012 it had 40 million users who were uploading a million photos a day. The company will continue to operate as a separate entity from Facebook and has become the most downloaded app for smartphones.[7]

Internet games, which we'll get into more in the next chapter, are games that people play on their computers or smartphones with more and more playing on the Internet with and against other gamers. These complex and massive multi-player games, with the most sophisticated graphics, are often played with and against others they meet casually on the websites of these games. For younger kids, we might be talking about games like KidZui. For older kids, we are talking about games like Words with Friends, Mafia Wars, or "Endless" that is described as "a unique fantasy 2D MMORPG in which you can become rich and famous, fight evil monsters, become a hero, or live as a normal citizen." MMORPGs (Massively Multiplayer Online Role-Playing Games) are where a large number of players interact with one another virtually.

According to the Entertainment Software Association, 190 million U.S. households will use a next-generation video game console in 2012 with the average U.S. household owning at least one dedicated game console, PC or smartphone. With next generation video game consoles, 148 million households will have this console connected to the Internet. While a majority of game players are over the age of 30, according to the trade association, 32 percent are under 18. In addition, 15 percent of the most frequent game players pay to play online games.[8]

Facebook has gotten so large, and for many users, even teens, so unwieldy, that something of a movement away from it has begun. It's certainly not a stampede, but it is something you should be aware of. While competition to see who has the most "friends" is still all the rage for many young users of Facebook it has become a chore to divide up all those friends into smaller groups and decide who should see what information. So the response has begun to move to smaller social networking sites. Several such as Path and Pair limit access to smartphones only. But as more and more users access social networks only via smartphone, that is not an impediment. Path limits users to 150 friends. Pair is exactly what the name implies—you are limited to one other person—the smallest of all possible friends' lists. This trend is likely to grow, and more and more teens will maintain accounts on multiple social networking sites.

Now that you know a bit about social networking, let's discuss the dangers of social networking.

PRIVACY AROUND SOCIAL NETWORKING

Social networking, whether via Facebook, Google+, texting, or Twitter by definition requires the user to give up some measure of his or her privacy. But privacy is central to making social media safe. Ask this broad question: Can social media and privacy ever coexist? The answer: probably not, or at least not without some effort. Social media, by its very nature, involves the sharing with others of easily transmitted or retransmitted data. This is almost the antithesis of privacy. Sharing and privacy can be viewed as polar opposites. But they can, and they have to, coexist. At the very least, we need to be able to control what we share and with whom—and to have a high degree of confidence that the information is protected.

If a computer user, be it an adult of a child, can keep their private information safe then they have won half the battle. But, as we shall see, it is not an altogether easy battle to wage let alone win. When talking about child identity theft, it is a battle that must be fought both by the child and by the parent. It requires the full cooperation of the child, the understanding of the parent as to how and where on the Internet the child or young person is active, and requires the young user of social media or online games to understand the potential danger of divulging personal information. Your children must be active participants in protecting their own privacy.

What exactly are the kinds of data that needs to be protected? The following list of personal individually identifiable information about an individual that might be found online seems fairly common:

- » A first and last name;

- » A home or other physical address including street name and name of a city or town;

- » An email address or other online contact information, including, but not limited to, user ID or screen name;

- » A telephone number;

- » A Social Security number;

- » A photograph.

Many young Facebook users like to get birthday wishes on their Facebook wall, so they list their birthdays. But cyber-security researchers at Carnegie Mellon University say you should never use your real birthday or hometown on your Facebook page. They discovered that if your Social Security number was issued before the new randomizing, a formula can figure out your Social Security number with just your birthday and your birth state.[9]

Your child needs to understand that posting any of these bits of personal information is potentially dangerous. If they do, they have to think twice or maybe three times before doing so, and then only do so in an environment they control access to such as behind a privacy wall that limits who can see the information.

As a parent, you are absolutely obligated to know what sites your child is visiting, how those sites work, what is the privacy policy of each site, how you set privacy controls on each site, and whether your child has those privacy safeguards in place.

In the case of younger children, many if not most of the most commonly visited and utilized sites, offer varying degrees of parental controls. You have an obligation to understand these controls and to use them to make your children safer.

Marc Rotenberg, Executive Director of the Electronic Privacy Information Center, told the Senate Committee on Commerce, Science, and Transportation Subcommittee on Consumer Protection, Product Safety, and Insurance of his concern that Facebook and other social networks sometimes manipulate privacy policies and settings to confuse users, extract more personal information from them, and then transfer the information to application developers and websites.[10]

> "We also see the increasingly opaque way that companies transfer user information to third parties. On the one hand, there is a great deal of transparency when users are able to see what they post and to make decisions about who should have access. On the other, the transfer of user data to application developers and now to websites is not so easy for users to observe and control. More specifically, there is

growing concern that companies are manipulating their privacy policies and privacy settings of users to confuse and frustrate users so that more personal information will be revealed."

More recently, he told another Senate subcommittee:

"There is no issue of greater concern to Internet users today than protecting the privacy and security of personal information. . . . Despite the recent Federal Trade Commission settlements, Google and Facebook continue to change their business practices in ways that lessen the ability of users to control their information. For example, Facebook launched Timeline, which made personal information that users thought had "vanished" suddenly available online. Users had to go back through their postings to remove wall posts that might be inappropriate or embarrassing."[11]

GAINING YOUR KIDS' COOPERATION

Here comes the part about making your children understand the dangers that lurk on the Internet and gaining their cooperation. You are going to need to talk with your children and you are going to have to make them understand you are not trying to snoop into their lives but are trying to keep them safe. You need to be partners in this effort, not adversaries. In an upcoming section, we'll try to help you at least get these conversations started.

Keeping children safe on the Internet, and protecting their data is one area that the federal government wants to help you as a parent. For instance here is some advice that the Federal Trade Commission gives:

CHECK OUT SITES YOUR KIDS VISIT

If a site requires users to register, see what kind of information it asks for and determine your comfort level. You also can see whether the site appears to be following the most basic rules, like posting its privacy policy for parents clearly and conspicuously.

REVIEW THE PRIVACY POLICY

Just because a site has a privacy policy doesn't mean it keeps personal information private. The policy can help you figure out if you're comfortable with what information the site collects and how it plans to use or share it. If the policy says there are no limits to what it collects or who gets to see it, there are no limits.

ASK QUESTIONS

If you have questions about a site's practices or policies, ask. The privacy policy should include contact information for someone prepared to answer your questions.

THE COMPANY BEHIND THE SITE

The privacy policy, in fact the whole operation of any website, is only as good and as reliable as the company behind the site. Make sure you and your children know who[12] these companies are and that your children are cognizant of going to reputable sites.

As a parent whose child is active using social media or spends time on the Internet, you need to become very familiar with COPPA—The Children's Online Privacy Protection Act—and your rights under this federal law.[13]

COPPA became effective April 21, 2000, and it gives the Federal Trade Commission the authority over the online collection of personal information from children under 13. It requires all websites who collect data from users under the age of 13, to have and to post a privacy policy. They must detail when and how they seek verifiable consent from a parent to allow the child under 13 to gain access to the site and to and participate in the site's activities. Finally, they must detail what responsibilities the site operator has and what's in place to protect children's privacy and safety online.

COPPA applies to individually personally identifiable information about a child such as full name, home address, email address, telephone number, or any other information that would allow someone to identify or contact the child. It also covers other types of information collected through cookies or tracking mechanisms—when they are tied to personally identifiable information.

The privacy policy is foremost, and it must provide details about the kind of information the site collects and what it will do with the information—such as sell it to advertisers. If the information is shared (or sold to) a third party, that entity must provide information on how it safeguards the data.

COPPA also gives parents the right to review whatever information a site has gathered on their children. Then, in one of more controversial aspects of this regulation, the site may chose to simply delete the information rather than show you. Conversely, you have the right to withdraw your consent to allowing your child access to the site and to demand any collected information be deleted.

School and school systems are exempted from COPPA. In addition, schools and school systems are allowed to stand in the place of parents to give permission for students to access website they utilize in the normal course of the education system. So parents should ask their children's schools what websites are used in the classrooms and find out whether those sites collect individual information on the student users.

Note that this federal protection applies only to information collected from users under the age of 13. The Web industry fought like tigers to keep the law from applying to all under the age of 18, which many in Congress wanted. That is why websites such as Facebook theoretically close their sites to all under the age of 13.

It is also important to note that COPPA does not prevent children under age 13 from accessing or participating in any social media websites. Rather, it adds requirements for any site operator who collects information on children under age 13. The most commonly heard complaint from web operators is what happens if they inadvertently collect data from users who are under 13. Many website operators try to be strict in not allowing those under 13 to have access to the site; however, understanding it will happen they try to protect themselves by extending many of the safeguards and protections offered to those under 13 to all site users who are under the age of 18.

Since COPPA's enactment in 2000, the rule has been aggressively enforced by the Federal Trade Commission. It has brought numerous enforcement actions against website operators and has collected a multi-million dollar fine and settlements for noncompliance. As this is writing, the Federal Trade Commission is proposing numerous revisions to COPPA in an effort to allow the rule to keep pace with changes in technology and to address what it sees as weaknesses in the present law.[14]

Many of these changes are very technical in nature, but one addresses the requirement of parental approval for access to sites that might collect information from children under age 13. The Federal Trade Commission proposes significant changes regarding obtaining verifiable parental consent. Currently website operators "must make reasonable efforts to obtain verifiable parental consent, taking into consideration available technology. Any method to obtain verifiable parental consent must be reasonably calculated in light of available technology to ensure that the person providing consent is the child's parent."[15]

One way to do this is by requiring a parent to use a credit card in connection with a transaction. Now the Federal Trade Commission wants to add several new methods including electronic scans of signed parental consent forms, video conferencing, and use of government-issued identification (such as a driver's license), while requiring the parent's ID information to be promptly deleted after verification is complete.

But even with proposed changes, the COPPA rule does not address the basic issue that kids lie, sometimes with the full knowledge of their parents. Parents let their kids under the age of 13 access sites that are age restricted either because the kids beg them or because they believe these sites offer educational or entertainment advantages for the child.

Generally speaking, it is up to the parent to know what websites their children are visiting and this is true whether your kid is eight or 12 or 15. Next the parents themselves should visit the sites, should read the privacy policies of those sites—and all have them prominently displayed. Then you need to sit down with your child and discuss how the child will use the site, what information will be shared, and then your child must be made to understand the potential consequences they could face should they unwisely use the site.

FACEBOOK

It will probably come as a shock to your kids, but Facebook is not some charitable entity that gives them a free platform to meet with and share all sorts of information with their friends. Facebook is a business and not just any business. It is a massive business with a massive valuation and massive potential to be "the" platform by which we all communicate. It's been hard to miss the recent attention given to Facebook's Initial Public Offering, which valued the company at more than $100 billion. What makes it so valuable? Simply put, its 800 million plus members worldwide and its unusual business plan, which differs significantly from its competitors.

Those competitors say they will make money by placing advertising in front of users in much the same way television delivers viewers to advertisers' commercials; probably not as blatantly, but much in the same ways. Facebook's vast potential worth, however, is derived from its ability to deliver very detailed information about its members to advertisers. Not information in general, but very specifically detailed information about individual users, and then selling that information to interested marketers and advertisers.

As we write this book, there are multiple bills bouncing around in Congress that attempt to increase Internet privacy and possibly limit what information websites can gather on their users. Some are specifically aimed at increasing privacy options for young people.

In anticipation of the eventual passage of a new law, Facebook is revising some of its privacy policies. These policies are not necessarily limiting what information it gathers but, instead, are giving users better access to see what information has been gathered about them.

Let's take Jenny Smith for example. Jenny is a Facebook member. Given the companies she has friended, the places she visits, the groups she has joined, it is obvious that Jenny is interested in weight loss and healthy eating. How valuable then is it to advertisers of exercise programs, weight-loss schemes, diet beverages, etc., to learn about Jenny, and how she can be reached. One targeted ad is worth thousands of randomly placed ads. Now, multiply Jenny by several million members, all potential consumers, and you begin to understand how Facebook can be valued at upward of $100 billion.

But Facebook knows more about Jenny than simply that she is interested in weight control and healthy eating. They know who her friends are, or were in the event she has defriended people. They know the identities of everyone who has asked to be her friend, even those she has ignored or denied. They know the IP addresses of every computer she has used to connect with Facebook. And, of course, they have copies of every post, every message, every photo she has posted and every conversation she has had through Facebook.

Facebook has been waging a battle in Europe with the European Union. One European Union researcher looked at the file that Facebook keeps on him and found the information was divided into 57 different categories. Some examples reportedly found were various categories of personal information such as name, name changes, alternative names, address, date of birth, gender, phone numbers, home town, places lived, and photo to financial information such as currency used, credit cards, work history to such things as friends, linked accounts, major life events, and favorite quotes.[16]

The company has the potential of delivering to advertisers huge numbers of potential customers screened to a level previously unimaginable. This is what makes Facebook potentially one of the most valuable companies on earth.

But it's also what makes Facebook potentially so dangerous for its members. Facebook members are so willing to post so much information about themselves that they open themselves to all sorts of dangers.

Here is a simple question to ask your kids: Who owns all the stuff they post on their Facebook page—the pictures, the messages, and the data that flies back and forth among "friends?" Who owns them? It seems almost a silly question with the seemingly obvious answer, "Why I own them, of course!"

Well, not exactly.

Read if you will, and make your kids read, Facebook's "Terms of Service." It's kind of a tough slog, but the rules make clear that even though you technically "own" what you post, the very act of posting gives Facebook "a non-exclusive, transferable, sub-licensable, royalty-free, worldwide license to use any IP (Intellectual Property—anything you create be it writing, photo, video, etc.) content that you post." In other words, yes, you own it but you are giving them the right to use it in any way they deem fit, and they don't have to pay you if they use it or even if they sell it.

Next, have your kids go to http://www.openbook.org. This is a website that allows you to search within Facebook. You can search by name, search by topic or search by content, i.e. "my teacher is a jerk." See exactly what Openbook says: "Facebook® helps you connect and share with the people in your life. Now, even if they are not your friends and you don't know them, you can still read people's recent posts (based on their own words)." This pretty much means what it says. Even if Facebook doesn't sell or distribute or use your content in an ad, it could easily end up on another site like Openbook or it can be downloaded by anyone you have friended who has access to your Facebook page and redistributed by that person at will.

Most of the experts agree, if a person has problems on Facebook, they have only themselves to blame. They likely openly post too much personal information about themselves and they don't take advantage of the privacy protections that Facebook offers. Therefore this personal information is available for one and all to see, and that is what leads to all sorts of problems.

If you have a teenage daughter, you might like to share with her this very real Facebook horror story. George Bronk, 23, from California faces six years in jail for hacking into the Facebook accounts of women, resetting their passwords, gaining access to their email accounts, searching for nude photos they may have sexted to friends and then putting those photos out into general circulation.[17]

According to newspaper accounts, Bronk acquired the pictures by searching Facebook for women who included on their public pages their email addresses, and seemingly innocuous personal information such as their pets' names, where they went to high school, their favorite foods, and the like. He used this data to guess passwords or answer questions sites used as security questions to test persons seeking entrance to email accounts and, once in, he took over the email account. He then searched for compromising photos.

In some cases, he sent the pictures to everyone in the victim's address book. In other cases, he threatened to make the pictures public unless the women sent even more explicit images. He told one woman he did it "because it was funny."

In pleading guilty in Sacramento Superior Court, he admitted to hacking into more than 3,200 email accounts and finding nude or semi-nude photos in 172 of them. Bronk was charged with felony hacking, child pornography, and identity theft charges.

What this amounts to is a cautionary tale on a number of different levels. The first deals with utilizing Facebook's privacy settings. To a certain extent, it exemplifies warnings you see from every expert. If your Facebook page is hacked or hijacked, in great measure you have only yourself to blame. You have not been careful about what you have posted or how you have posted it. Likely, you thought nothing of posting or talking about your full name, birth date, addresses, phone numbers, and the names of relatives. But to an open audience, it is just enough to allow your identity to the stolen or your Facebook page hacked.

Of course, the Bronk saga serves as a cautionary tale of the dangers of posting on the Internet or emailing any kind of picture you don't want the whole wold to see.

"S," as well call her, was feeling a bit mean one day and posted a picture of herself and who soon would no longer be her best friend because the picture of the friend was, to say the least, unflattering. The friend quickly complained and S came to her senses and quickly took the picture down. But by that time, several others in her class had seen it and downloaded it, and reposted it everywhere. So now her friend, her former friend, was being laughed at by everyone.

The moral here, as it was with the women who had kept suggestive pictures of themselves in their email or in their files, is what you post, or send, can never be really taken back.

Let's go back for a moment to a statement I made a bit ago: Kids lie. As far as Facebook use is concerned, I have seen a pair of eye-opening studies.

The first is from "MinorMonitor," a company that allows parents to monitor their children's use of Facebook and other social media sites. Given the obvious potential bias, or perhaps self-interest, in most of what the study found, you could take some of these numbers with a grain of salt. But the findings here are mirrored in other studies from clearly unbiased sources.

MinorMonitor surveyed 1,000 parents about how their children use Facebook. Not surprisingly, it concluded that 38 percent of children using Facebook are under 13; rather shockingly, 40 of these children were under the age of six.[18]

More than half of parents responding monitor their children's Facebook use by logging into their accounts; while one-quarter keep tabs by "friending" their children. Eight percent make their children show them their profile page. Seventeen percent don't track their children's use of Facebook at all, which is still way too many.

Given the tool that MinorMonitor is selling, you might question some of these findings. They are also echoed in a study done by the highly respected Consumer Reports organization and released in the summer of 2011.

Consumer Reports found that, of the 20 million minors who actively used Facebook in the past year, 7.5 million—or more than one-third—were younger than 13, "and not supposed to be able to use the site." Moreover, more than five million were age 10 and under, "and their accounts were largely unsupervised by their parents."[19]

This latter claim probably needs more exploration. But Consumer Reports' conclusion is the younger the user, the greater likelihood the child's use is not being monitored by an adult.

"Parents of kids 10 and younger on Facebook seem to be largely unconcerned. Only 18 percent made their child a Facebook friend, which is the best way to monitor the child. By comparison, 62 percent of parents of 13- to 14-year-olds did so. Only 10 percent of parents of kids 10 and under had frank talks about appropriate online behavior and threats."

To us, this is inconceivable, although there is a kind of logic to it. Parents of younger children might think them less likely to take risks or expose themselves to online threats than older children. What harm can a 10-year-old get into? Well, the answer is a lot of harm, not the least of which is infecting the home network with a virus they have let into the system.

Another recent study startled us. According to a survey conducted by Microsoft Research, more than half of 1,007 parents surveyed knew their 12-year-olds (or younger) have a Facebook account and more than three-fourths of these either knew when their underage children joined Facebook and/or helped them create the account.[20]

But most of all, many of the parents in the survey said they didn't even know Facebook had an age restriction—and only a few who those who knew realized it was federal law.

Let's revisit the federal COPPA law and the Federal Trade Commission's regulations. If literally millions of young people under the COPPA's statutory age limit of 13 are using Facebook, regardless of what the site's regulations are, shouldn't COPPA apply to Facebook?

Sites where personal information by users under 13 can be publicly viewed violate the COPPA regulations. COPPA prohibits sites from knowingly disclosing children's personally identifiable information.

Facebook argues several things in the alternative. They say, quite correctly, that kids lie and they can't be held responsible. They also argue that many of the requirements of protections under COPPA are already present on their site and de facto they are abiding by the regulations. Critics demand that the age limit on COPPA be raised to 18, but the whole social media world is fighting that one.

Facebook creator Mark Zuckerberg says he believes it is important that younger children be able to use the site for educational purposes. Facebook says it removes "many underage accounts each day" and is supportive of "federal efforts to modernize COPPA so that companies can innovate and keep young people of all ages safe online." But "modernization" does not extend to raising the age COPPA covers to under 18.[21]

Facebook has had its share of problems. The Federal Trade Commission announced a broad settlement that required the company to respect the privacy wishes of its users and subjects it to audits for the next 20 years. The order, which claimed Facebook engaged in "unfair and deceptive" practices, was based on the way Facebook handled information its users deemed to be private information.

So kids lie to get on Facebook, and when those "liars" start to number in the millions, critics say, the problem rests with how easy it is to sign up to use Facebook.

Facebook screens applicants by asking for their birth date and rejecting those too young. But someone under 13 can join by simply falsifying their birth date. Joining Facebook doesn't require registering with a credit card, though, as we saw, that is one of the tests under COPPA that can be used to weed out the underage. If Facebook required a credit card to register, or one of the other forms of verification likely to be slowed under the proposed COPPA revisions, even if nothing is charged against the card, it would limit the numbers of minors illegally gaining entry.

Facebook argues against this, saying a credit card requirement would close entry from adults in the lower economic strata. Then, too, kids seeking entrance could simply make up credit card numbers unless each was checked against the applicant for relevance. This is, of course, a path that Facebook could take, albeit at the expense of collecting and safely storing the credit card numbers.

Under the changes to COPPA proposed by the Federal Trade Commission, one would expand the definition of "personal information" to first include any identifier that permits physical or online contacting of a specific individual and then any photographs, videos, and audio files, regardless of whether they are combined with a child's name or contact information. Currently, the COPPA rule deems a photograph to be personal information only if it is combined with other information that permits the physical or online contacting of the child. COPPA hasn't kept up with Facebook and YouTube so it doesn't protect what's in a video or audio format.[22]

As parents, we have an obligation to effectively monitor our kids' usage of Facebook and other social media sites. A starting point would seem to be using the sites directly, for ourselves. The next step would be to understand the privacy policies and how their privacy controls work. Remember, at the heart of Facebook's existence, and central to its business model, is the collection of data about its millions of users not in the abstract, not in general, but information specific to each user. Thus, critics charge, the whole system of privacy controls are made difficult and more than a bit obtuse, but if your kids are using Facebook, you have to master it as well.

Let's first look at what you need to access your kids' Facebook page. Much advice, and it's good advice, is that you need to "friend" your kids. With that level of access you will see what their friends see. But if your kids are younger, and certainly if they are in their early or mid-teens, you might want greater access. You need to know their passwords so you can go onto Facebook as them and see everything on their page. This should be your bottom line. No password, no Facebook.

As they grow older, it's obviously going to be progressively more difficult to expect your kids to give you password access to their Facebook page. At this point, maybe it will be enough to be a "friend." By this time, if you have worked with them, they will understand the danger that lurks out there and will be more responsible in what they post and how they post it.

For younger children, it is advisable to use your email address as the contact for their account so that you receive their notifications and are better able to monitor their activities. Again, this is a situation that is easier for a 13-year-old than a 17-year-old.

It needs to be noted that Facebook is a very deep and very complex website. We simply don't have room here to discuss all of the potential dangers. This is even truer now that Facebook has introduced features like Timeline, which chronologically assembles, displays, and makes globally accessible the preferences, acquaintances, and activities of members. Then, there is the "ticker," which shows what your friends are doing and allows you to eavesdrop when one of your friends says something (and allows others to eavesdrop on you).

Here are some key things that should be addressed to minimize your children's exposure:

Login/password information: On the one hand, parents should have access to their children's login and password information. At the same time, children must be taught to safeguard that information—to never give it out, especially to strangers who may ask for it online, even if they pose as authority figures representing the website.

At IDENTITY GUARD®, we work with bloggers to help promote our child identity theft protection service, IDENTITY GUARD® KID SURE[SM]. One of those bloggers, KID SURE[SM] Ambassador Kris Cain, writes a blog (http://www.LittleTechGirl.com) and gives some very good advice about passwords not only for kids, but ones that we adults can take to heart.

> "I set a password on each and gave it to them. They are not the hardest passwords ever due to their nine-year-old memories, but they do follow my password rules. As they use more websites and get more accounts, I want to make sure that they know the makings of a good password."

DON'TS:

- » Never make your password your name
- » Never make your password or PIN your birthday
- » Never make your password too short
- » Never make your password something that those close to you can guess easily
- » Never carry your passwords with you

DOS:

- » Do make your password very secure
- » Do mix letters and numbers to create an effective password
- » If you do want to use a play on names, make sure to mix it up with a play on numbers as letters, etc.
- » Do have different passwords for very important things like your bank account and your utility bills
- » Do use separate passwords for things work-related versus personal

Another KID SURE[SM] Ambassador, Erica Mueller (http://www.ericasays.com) has come up with an interesting way of devising a complex password that meets most any website's requirements as to length and types of characters that are included, yet is easy enough for a pre-teen to remember without having to write it down.

She starts by inventing an easy to remember phrase—in this example: "Chocolate Ice Cream Rocks" and takes the first letter of each word: CIR as the first three letters of the password. Then she adds the name of the website, a special character and her birth year ending up with the password "CIR(all caps)facebook@84."

SHE SAYS:

> "What you've ended up with is an alphanumeric password with both upper and lowercase letters and a special character. This is considered a very strong password. Many sites require all of these be present when you create a password, so it's great if you've already established this habit and you're not having to come up with a new password that you may not remember, just because you've landed on a site with these requirements. Another thing to note is most sites require an 8- (sometimes 12-) character minimum for passwords."

Privacy Settings: A user's basic information—a potential goldmine for an identity thief—is kept in a user's "profile." This profile has levels of privacy available and children must be taught how to keep their profiles private. If the child makes the profile public, it can be viewed by anyone. You can limit access to profile information to only yourself, friends, or to friends of friends— which is probably a bad idea. You can limit access to items such as photos, or block specific people from seeing them or give access only to certain people or groups. Thus, a parent must often check that their children's profiles are being kept private. You also must make sure your kids have not blocked you. At the same time your children should limit the amount of personal information contained in a profile, even if it's kept private. They should leave out contact information, such as phone number and address and they should leave out full birthdays. A bottom line: if you want to stop strangers from seeing everything you do, you and your friends need to change your privacy settings to "friends" or custom lists.

Friending/Defriending: We can't say this often enough, nor more strongly—kids must be made to understand they cannot accept friend requests from strangers. Many kids enter into contests to see who can amass the most friends. This exposes their private information to one and all. Identity thieves troll Facebook trying to become friended by strangers to steal data. Many brag that once accepted as a friend they can steal an identity in a matter of minutes. Your kids must understand they need to decline anyone they don't know. They might lose the friending contest, but they will stay safer. They also need to understand that when you "defriend" someone, they still stay subscribed to your public posts. If you want to defriend and don't want them to see posts, then you have to also block them.

Chat: Facebook's "chat" feature allows users to talk with others while on the site. Parents must make sure the feature is turned off to protect younger children. Just as they check privacy control levels, parents should check that chat remains turned off. Older children will probably resist and want to use chat, but they have to be made to understand the dangers in talking with people they don't know.

Commenting: You should also check a post's security level before you comment on it. There is a small icon under each item and a globe icon means it is public and viewable by anyone. Also realize that any comment on a public post will be sent to the Tickers of every person on your friend list.

Photos: There can be multiple dangers in the posting of photos. Even the most innocent photos can give away information or can possibly be used by predators. Parents should decide if they want their kids posting photos and if so perhaps to limit them to photos of their faces only.

Search Engines: Another important privacy setting rests in the search section of Facebook's privacy controls. To prevent strangers from accessing your page through search engines, the box "Only Friends" for Facebook search results should be checked and the box for public search results should not be checked. This is another item parents must frequently confirm.

Monitoring your kids' use of Facebook can be difficult and time-consuming, it's for that reason you might want to employ one of a number of parental control software programs that will make this task both easier and surer.

PARENTAL CONTROL SOFTWARE CAN ALLOW PARENTS TO DO SEVERAL THINGS:

- » Manage time spent on the Internet or on the computer
- » Limit what their children are allowed to see and read online
- » Select which computer programs children can use
- » Monitor and log all Internet activity

Many of these programs allow parents to have unlimited access to what their children are doing while on the website. You likely will face resistance from your kids if you employ such a program, but the simple answer is this is the price they pay for Facebook access.

Google+—Google says Google+ is different from other social networking sites (read Facebook) in that it provides more tools for users to meet and interact with new people that have similar interests as their own. It is also different, it says, in the fact it has automated many of the tasks that you have to do on other social networking sites (read Facebook). Does this sound to you like potential problems for young users? It does to us.

One thing Google+ does offer is more privacy options and more specific privacy options allowing users to hide data without hiding an entire profile, as an example. It also allows for more options as to who can see what piece of data that has been posted.

In Google+ "profiles," the basic information users post about themselves, user screen names and photos are always public, but the site offers a number of privacy settings for restricting or hiding other profile information.

In Google+, you organize your all your contacts into "circles" (the equivalent of Facebook's groups or friend list). You can have a circle for family members, one for school friends, one for friends from church, etc. You can have as many different circles as you want, and you can call them anything you want.

Google+ gives the user that ability to control what content is shown to which circle and the ability to essentially create a sub-circle within a circle and make more content available to this sub-group. One clear advantage is that Google+ allows users to control who can tag (identify and thus make available to a search) them in photos, as opposed to Facebook, which only allows users to hide tags after they have been created and most likely in circulation.

A specific danger in Google+ is that your username and your photo are always public, so you must take care not to post anything more than a headshot rather than a photo filled with your friends or your family. Within this greater ability to find other users with common interests, Google+ makes it much easier for even strangers to follow you but they are limited to seeing only what you have posted and made public.

When Google+ went online in June of 2011, access was limited to those 18 and older. The site authors then concentrated on privacy issues and essentially reversed privacy controls for those ages 13 to 17. Whereas adults have to turn on various privacy protections in Google+, if when you register and indicate you are between the ages 13 and 17, the highest level of privacy becomes the default.

In the user profile, for example, there is a section on education and one on employment. In an adult user's profile, the default is so anyone can view these sections, just as anyone can view the "relationship status" section. With young people, only those within their circles can view these sections.

Then there is the question of who can post messages to a specific user. The default for those over 18 is "anyone." But, for young people, the default changes to the opposite end of the scale—only those in your circles. Likewise, for adult users, the default is that "anyone" can comment of a public post by the user, but for young people the default becomes only those in their circles.

There are safeguards built into usage by those between the ages of 13 and 17. If a young user posts something that is intended for what is called an "extended" circle or for the general public, a warning pops up that says, "When you share to your extended circles, people you haven't added to your circles will be able to view your post and may be able to comment."

While Google+ can seem safer out of the box then say Facebook, it is possible for a young user to make most, if not all, their settings less restrictive and the data more accessible, just as an adult can change their settings to make data more restrictive. In fact, it may be too easy for a young person to defeat some of the key safeguards that Google+ has put into place.

This once again brings us to the central fact regarding how to stay safe on Google+. You have to use the privacy settings correctly, and it is up to parents to make sure those privacy settings are as strong as possible, and are in constant use.

In the end, what it all comes down to is taking the time to find out what social media or gaming websites your children are visiting and using, how those websites work, including all security options and protection, and staying in contact with their usage of social media to keep them safe. Like having a conversation about the birds and bees, we need to talk with our children about social media and Internet safety and help them to understand that staying safe is for their own good. In a bit, I'll try to give you some ideas how to approach these modern day birds and bees conversations, but first, let's talk about a couple other places where your kids can be exposed—mobile technology and gaming.

CHAPTER SEVEN:

EXPOSED AT PLAY

Welcome to the newest parental dilemma of the twenty-first century. The pleading usually starts at about age maybe age 10 if you're lucky. "Mom and Dad, can I pleassseee have a cell phone? All of my friends have them . . . I'll use it responsibly and it's for my safety. You can always get in touch with me. I'll have it in case of any emergency. Pah-leeeeaaasssee!"

This is only the first part of a three-part drama. Part one: Should I get him or her a cell phone? Part two: How "smart" should that cell phone be? Part three: How do I balance my child's privacy and independence against my need to keep them safe?

Part one depends on your child, their maturity level, and your mutual need for them to have a cell phone for practical reasons. You need and want them to be able to get in touch with you (and vice versa) quickly and easily. Part one, therefore, has been resolved and is completely rational. You have decided to provide your child with a cell phone.

I have chosen one word in the previous sentence with some care—provide. It is an important word because it should govern your whole relationship with your kids regarding cell phones. Unless your child is working and paying for the phone themselves, you are providing it. Whether it is part of a family plan with your own cell carrier, or a separate plan including pay as you go, you are providing it so, in other words, it is not "their" cell phone, but it is yours, and you can and should control its usage not just for financial reasons, but also keeping your kids safe.

Now comes part two: "I need to be able to text you and look stuff up on the Internet!" they insist. They will also tell you that they need unlimited texting because you'll want to send them texts—perhaps while they are in class—so they can call back right after school. Besides, as they will tell you at great length, what's the good of a phone without texting . . . all my friends text, older siblings text. So you put the new phone on the family plan with unlimited texting. Now the next part of this drama, how "smart" should their phone be?

Obviously a plain old cell phone, one that simply sends and receives calls, is the safest kind of phone to get. But it will not have the ability to browse the Internet and may even have limited (or clunky) texting capabilities, so your kids will tell you "why bother." Moreover, plain vanilla cell phones are becoming a lot less common these days.

Now you've made the decisions to provide your child with a smartphone. The next logical question becomes, "How smart?" Remember, a smartphone, be it as smart as the iPhone 4S or one of the new sleek phones utilizing Google's Android operating system is basically a handheld computer and some even have more computing power as a desktop or notebook. It is a powerful device and one that can cause a lot of problems for your child and for you if operated carelessly or recklessly.

Now the most important part: How do you keep your child safe when using a smartphone?

Before you get this phone, you need to look at some things. First and foremost, does the phone's operating system come with a parental control function, one that can put a lock on any number of phone functions? Does the parental control function utilize a password that the parent sets and once set can only be changed using a password to gain entry? If not, under no circumstances should you buy the phone. Don't use a password that you use elsewhere, or one that your child might have learned. Moreover, don't use one that can be easily guessed. If the child can get access to the parental control function and change the settings, you might as well have never set them in the first place.

Secondly, most smartphones today come equipped with cameras. Many also come equipped with GPS technology. The combination poses a simply unacceptable risk. Unless settings are adjusted properly, when a photo is taken by the phone's camera, it is "geotagged." This means that data providing longitude and latitude of where the photo or video was taken is attached to the photo, and in some cases ownership information is taken from the phone's setup system. Potentially, that photo, which has been circulated to friends or within a circle can be reposted in a more public fashion, and the geotag can be read, exposing your child to all kinds of dangers.

One example: You take and post a picture from in front of your house. It can be very innocent—just a quick snap of a group of friends playing around and taken with your smartphone and put on your Facebook page for other friends to see. But that photo now contains information about exactly where the photo was taken—in this case exactly where you live. That is information you do not want in the wrong hands.

Other similar innocent photos can tell where you spend time out of the house—your favorite mall or park, for instance—or it can tell when you are home alone or actually when the house is empty.

> "I'd say very few people know about geotag capabilities," said Peter Eckersley, a staff technologist with the Electronic Frontier Foundation in San Francisco, "and consent is sort of a slippery slope when the only way you can turn off the function on your smartphone is through an invisible menu that no one really knows about."[1]

On many phones, turning off the geotag function is quite difficult. It's relatively easy to turn off all location features, but in doing so you eliminate some of a smartphone's most valuable features like step-by-step mapping. So the trick is to keep the location features that benefit you while disabling geotagging. A very useful website is http://www.ICanStalkU.com helps you figure out how you are vulnerable and lets you disable geotagging. This site also lists specific instructions to deactivate geotagging on a wide range of smartphones. In addition, there is now software that can search your computer for geotags on photos, and remove the information so you can repost the pictures geotag free.

Does the phone you are contemplating for your child come with "Bluetooth" capability? Bluetooth technology enables a mobile phone or device to find and "talk" to other bluetooth-enabled mobile devices in close proximity. This means if your child's mobile device has its Bluetooth functionality turned on, your child's phone or device can receive unwanted calls or messages from other Bluetooth-enabled devices and any personal information stored on your child's phone could be vulnerable to scammers. So if the phone or device you are contemplating is capable of Bluetooth, find out how this function be turned off under the password-protected parents-safety option.

Finally, does the phone or mobile device you are contemplating offer content controls that are set by parents? Almost without question, your child will be playing games on the device. Many offer a control system where the phone will be unable to access games that come rated for adult use only. As with other parental safety features some phones allow this feature to be turned on or off only through a password-protected feature.

Now comes the most difficult decision of all, how much and how to monitor your child's mobile device. "Don't you trust me?" Whether your child is eight or 16, you will hear some form of this question and the answer is probably different depending on the age of your child.

This quandary of how and how much to monitor your child's mobile phone use is a universal one for parents, and the answer probably differs from parent to parent for child to child from situation to situation. To us, it seems obvious that the young and more inexperienced the child the greater is the need for monitoring. But the inverse is the simple fact that the older the child, the greater are the potential dangers they face.

What should the parents' response be? One would be to sit the child down, provide some ground rules, and then follow up with frequent further discussions. Then the answer is one of complete trust. Somewhere in the middle is to take the child's phone or mobile device and, before handing it over, to set various levels of parental controls in a way the child cannot change. Lastly, at the far end of the scale is to install software on the phone or device that will control its use and theoretically increase its level of safety.

The British headquartered Vodafone, whose cell systems are active in many countries in Europe, Asia, and elsewhere in the world (but not the U.S.), is a leader in providing advice to parents and a way to ensure they can control the cell phone use of their children. Part of this extremely activist role is in response to some rather strict laws that are in effect throughout Europe that have been promulgated by the European Union.

One facet of Vodafone activist response is that they make available to parents perhaps the most encompassing parental control software I have seen. Vodafone Guardian is a free Android app that enables parents to protect children from inappropriate calls, messages, and online content. According to the company, by installing the app on their children's phone, they can configure their children's smartphones to block specific contacts or mobile phone numbers to prevent cyber-bullying text messages or calls. They can also transfer abusive or bullying text messages to a secure folder in the smartphone's onboard memory, which can be accessed by school authorities or even law enforcement.

The Vodafone app can also restrict outgoing calls to specified contacts only, and to specific times during the day and evening when calls can or cannot be made or received. Time limits can also be set for the use of specific apps. During "no calls or apps" periods, use of apps and all inbound or outbound calls can be blocked. Restrictions can also be applied on a contact-by-contact basis. These restrictions can be overridden to make emergency calls or calls to a specific number such as home or a parent's workplace.

The app also enables parents to block access to the mobile web at specific times, or at all times. The restrictions apply across all wireless networks, including 3G, wi-fi and Bluetooth. The app can also be used to deactivate the smartphone's camera all the time or at specific times.

Any number of domestic companies are rushing to develop similar types of parental control apps. For example, Symantec's Norton Online Family has allowed parents to monitor their kids' use of home computers. Using it allows parents to monitor their kids' social network activity including recording their kids' profile pages and any changes made to them. The program monitors instant messages sent and received and monitors many major chat services and tells you who your kids chat with and what they say. It monitors the computer's search functions and tracks the words, terms, and phrases your kids search for online, and it will send you an email when your kids do something they shouldn't.

Now this program can be—at least in part—monitoring what your kids do on their smartphones too. The Norton Safety Minder app lets parents see all the websites their kids visit, or attempt to visit, and allows parental blockage of specific sites or types of sites.

Another company offering a parental control app is Kaspersky Lab, maker of computer anti-virus software.

Kaspersky is developing a parental control application that is now in beta form and provides parents with the ability to manage how their children are using mobile phones and the content they are exposed to. The app features include web filtering, which blocks sites with inappropriate content, such as pornography, violence, and drugs. It also has application control capabilities that allow parents to control which applications can be run on their children's Android devices, and to control which contacts are allowed for communication, monitoring messaging logs, and specifying any personal information a parent may want blocked from transmitting.

A wide range of such programs will be available shortly. It's up to you to decide whether to utilize them.

But whether you do or not, and whether your child is eight or 16, certain things should be discussed with them if they are about to join the mobile world. One is online "chat."

You have probably already warned them about the dangers of chatting on your home computers, but many smartphones give them this ability from wherever they are. And what kid can resist this? You need to discuss online chatting with your child, whether age eight or sixteen, and you need to educate yourself about whether your child is simply chatting with friends or their own "circle" or whether their chats include strangers who they meet online, for instance, when they're playing a Massively multiplayer online role-playing game (MMORPG).

Parents must impress upon their children that when online chatting to never give out any personal information such as phone number, email address, or anything else that could divulge where they live or their real name.

You need to have something approaching an absolute rule. Forbid your child from meeting up in person with people they've met through online chats. If your child does want to meet with someone who they have chatted with online, perhaps they share a common interest or hobby, it is absolutely required you contact the other child's parents and go along to the meeting in a public place. The person they are meeting with should always be age-appropriate and never an adult.

Finally, you need to know and approve of the chat rooms your child is visiting, and be vigilant about ensuring that the chat rooms they are visiting are age appropriate. As a parent, you most likely have been very careful to know all of your children's friends in what I'll call "the physical world." When they were younger, this was fairly simple. It is more difficult as they get older, but you still try. Now, you have the added dimension of trying to keep track of their friends in the online world. Your goal as a parent is no different than it has been in keeping track of who they see or run around with in the physical world, it's just it is more difficult to do that in the cyber world. But you goal should be the same.

To learn 10 Ways to Protect
Your Smartphone, Laptop and Tablet
Visit
www.BankruptAtBirthBook.com

RISKS AND REALITIES OF OUR MOBILE WORLD

As more people have gotten wise to computer-based scams, scammers are now targeting people using mobile devices, and their prime targets are young people. The stark reality of users of mobile devices is that these users are three times more likely to fall for fake messages than computer users, according to several different online security firms.

As parents, if we allow our kids to utilize devices to text and tweet, our jobs are to make them less gullible, more suspicious, and more selfish with their information.

From the first day they were on a home computer, you surely have warned them never to respond to an email from someone they did not know. You have warned them never to download a file, a photo, or an attachment from someone they did not know. This same kind of warning must now be made and made again to ensure safe mobile device usage. But there is a difference. They must be on guard—not so much against downloading a virus, although that is possible—but for mobile devices, the dangers are innocently divulging personal information.

For instance, most people have a hard time resisting something that is advertised as "free." In this day and age, scammers have gotten more and more sophisticated. Now the new danger is the free app.

An email will appear in your inbox that looks very official from some entertainment giant or some well-known social media service. The invitation is hard to resist—just click here, it might say, and you will be immediately sent a new fun app that will allow you to do wondrous things … and it's all completely free! What kid can resist?

So your kid clicks and an app appears, but it just does not seem to work. Oh heck, your kids will probably think, it was free so it doesn't much matter. They likely won't give it a second thought.

But, here's the thing … the app is working, and what it's doing is capturing all the data on the smartphone and transmitting it to the scammer.

"It's very rare now where you find somebody dumpster diving to get someone's Social Security number. They really don't have to—they have the worldwide web," says FBI Supervisory Senior Resident Agent Mark Karangekis.

Apps, says Special Agent Karangekis are a new way for thieves to take your personal information. Once you download an app, look at what permissions it requests. The Gmail app can access your personal information and contact data. The Facebook app can access your location, your phone calls, and also your personal information. "You should be concerned about the personal information associated with your phone in general," says Karangekis.[2]

Some other tips from the FBI: Don't respond to phishing emails. The ones you may receive that appear to be from Paypal, Amazon, or other popular sites probably are not. Finally, leave your home address off the Internet, even for resume websites. Thieves could submit a change of address form and have your mail sent to their p.o. box. Maybe you and your kids will get lucky and discover that the mobile device has been set up properly—and by properly we mean again without the kind of personal data that the scammer is most searching for. Maybe all that's divulged will be your child's phone book, so their friends will quickly be getting their invitation to download the free app. But, at the very least, the scammer will now have your child's name, address, and phone number. Is this enough to allow their identity to be stolen? Hopefully not, but then only time will tell. Your child needs to eliminate even the possibility. Don't download any app unless you are absolutely sure of where you are getting it from and be sure that it's something you've initiated, not a response to an unsolicited invitation.

Once your kids have begun chatting with friends via text messaging or Twitter, where they are limited to 140 characters, they will begin using a language of acronyms and abbreviations.

You might start to see messages like: hi i'm vry bord 2nite u wnt2go sumwhr we cn HF. To you, this might as well be in Mandarin, but it is actually a very simple message meaning: hi I'm very bored tonight, you want to go somewhere we can have fun?

Whole books are being written about texting and tweeting lingo. Some of the lists we have seen now run 500-plus abbreviations. Erin Jansen at http://www. netlingo.com has compiled many top-50 lists of lingo used in the online world, including several she lists as ones that every parent should know. They are a bit too racy for this book. Another very useful site, http://www.lingo2word.com, contains a thorough dictionary and a translation tool for tranlating messages in lingo to proper English and vice versa. The following is one of Jansen's lists.

TOP 50 POPULAR TEXT & CHAT ACRONYMS:

1. 2moro—Tomorrow
2. 2nite—Tonight
3. BRB—Be Right Back
4. BTW—By The Way
5. B4N—Bye For Now
6. BCNU—Be Seeing You
7. BFF—Best Friends Forever
8. CYA—Cover Your Ass -or- See Ya
9. DBEYR—Don't Believe Everything You Read
10. DILLIGAS—Do I Look Like I Give A Sh**
11. FUD—Fear, Uncertainty, and Disinformation
12. FWIW—For What It's Worth
13. GR8—Great
14. ILY—I Love You
15. IMHO—In My Humble Opinion
16. IRL—In Real Life
17. ISO—In Search Of
18. J/K—Just Kidding
19. L8R—Later
20. LMAO—Laughing My Ass Off
21. LOL—Laughing Out Loud -or- Lots Of Love
22. LYLAS—Love You Like A Sister
23. MHOTY—My Hat's Off To You
24. NIMBY—Not In My Back Yard
25. NP—No Problem -or- Nosy Parents

26. NUB—New person to a site or game

27. OIC—Oh, I See

28. OMG—Oh My God

29. OT—Off Topic

30. POV—Point Of View

31. RBTL—Read Between The Lines

32. ROTFLMAO—Rolling On The Floor Laughing My Ass Off

33. RT—Real Time

34. THX or TX or THKS—Thanks

35. SH—Sh** Happens

36. SITD—Still In The Dark

37. SOL—Sh** Out of Luck

38. STBY—Sucks To Be You

39. SWAK—Sealed (or Sent) With A Kiss

40. TFH—Thread From Hell

41. RTM or RTFM—Read The Manual -or- Read The F***ing Manual

42. TLC—Tender Loving Care

43. TMI—Too Much Information

44. TTYL—Talk To You Later -or- Type To You Later

45. TYVM—Thank You Very Much

46. VBG—Very Big Grin

47. WEG—Wicked Evil Grin

48. WTF—What The F***

49. WYWH—Wish You Were Here

50. XOXO—Hugs and Kisses

We need also to talk about Internet gaming. Your child has likely played games on the computer since they were quite young. Many studies show that the computer, with its games, has become a babysitter for harried parents while they are trying to make dinner or complete chores around the house. So it is probable, at least we hope, that parents and their children have discussed some of the dangers inherent with Internet games.

Hopefully, you as parents are familiar with the types of games your child plays and one way to accomplish this is simply ask them to show you their favorite games and watch them as they play the game. You should reach an understanding about the types of games they can download.

Games today are rated much like movies—content appropriate for various ages. The Entertainment Software Rating Board (ESRB) rates almost every game on the market in a system that ranges from EC (early childhood) to E (everyone), E10+ (everyone over age ten), T (teen), M (mature 17+) to A (adult 18+).

If they are playing online with strangers, you should make sure the game and its players are age appropriate for your children. This is no different from your discussion and rules governing safe chatting.

Realize, too, that all this applies to their mobile devices and smartphones, which are really just small computers. Many of the games they can play on a home computer can also be played on their smartphones. You need to determine if those phones have content controls and if they are turned on. Also, if they are playing online games with strangers, you must determine who it is they are playing with.

A few final words about game controllers: These devices allow single or multiple players to compete in computer games. Whether it's Microsoft's Xbox 360, Nintendo's Wii or Sony's PLAYSTATION 3, most utilize controllers that have a parent-control function built it. You can, and I believe should, set the level by ratings the games your children are allowed to play.

You should realize that most controllers have the ability to connect users to the Internet, and they are playing games on sites owned by game makers. Many Internet-based games require users to register to play the games on the sites. The fee-based games, or even the ones that are free but that give "rewards" for attaining certain levels—usually admission to the next highest levels—establish user accounts that require users to provide private information. You need to ensure that your kids are not providing too much information to these web sites.

Game consoles such as Xbox are essentially computers. They store information like who who the players are, who's been chatting online, your message logs, and other online activity via the game console.

The Internet is filled with tips about how to hack various game controllers, which can allow users access to levels of games the controllers are theoretically programmed to lock out or allow users to play games for free when fees are being charged. But as parents, you need to worry about other kinds of hacking.

Spammers are perfecting ways to deliver malware via use of gaming sites by computer or game controller. In early 2012, Avast, a maker of computer software said it found 60 sites that contained "game" or "arcade" in their title, and if you connect to them you face the danger of Javascript infections, redirectors, and potentially unwanted software.[3]

Then too, there is the personal information your children have registered with game sites. This data is vulnerable to hacking. Recently, the Federal Trade Commission imposed a $250,000 civil penalty on the site http://wwww. RockYou.com for allowing hackers to access the personal information of 32 million users and violated the Children's Online Privacy Protection Act Rule (COPPA) in collecting information from approximately 179,000 children.[4]

In China, a popular game site, http://wwww.Duowan.com, was hacked, and the private information of 20 million users stolen.

Many of these games can be played on phones; in fact, most game sites now have versions written explicitly for smartphones. Game playing on smartphones contain all the dangers that online chatting does.

As parents, we need to first warn our kids and then become proactive in monitoring them not to invade their privacy, but to keep them safe.

CHAPTER EIGHT:

THE BIRDS & THE BEES 2.0

The concept of selective hearing applies to my two daughters, and perhaps it applies to your kids, too. In fact, I think that there's some physiological problem at my house because when I say "Emily, clean your room," nothing happens. I even get a little crazy and change it up from time to time and say, "Chase, clean your room," and still, nothing happens. There's no reaction from either of them.

You know the feeling?

So, the dilemma that we face is trying to figure out how to get our kids to listen. Sometimes we raise our voices, make idle threats, ground them, or even bribe them with ice cream. What's common in all of this is that it's usually the parents telling the kids to do something—be it their homework, cleaning their room, or not to talking to strangers. Rarely, is it the kids talking to other kids about such things.

Something very interesting happened several months ago on our way home from my daughter's lacrosse practice. We were driving a teammate to her house when she grabbed my daughter's Apple iPod Touch and asked her for her password. Without missing a beat, my daughter replied, "Sorry, I can't. My dad told me to never share my password."

So, after dropping off her friend, I told my daughter that I was very proud of her. I then said, "Ya know, it's always the parents who are telling our kids what to do. What if the kids told other kids what to do? I'll bet more kids would listen. What do you think?"

Several hours later, I was surprised to see my home office transformed into an imaginative store called "Sparkles." (I think it was meant to be some kind of clothing store because my clothes were draped on the desk, the shelving, and the chairs, and there was a hand-written sign that read "Sparkles" propped up on my desk.)

What I then discovered was that my daughter wrote a script about—you guessed it—identity theft. I was blown away. She not only had a script, but she had written lines for my youngest daughter who, in this story, was the cashier at Sparkles. She wanted to reenact just how easy it was to have an identity stolen.

The video that my daughter later compiled is about two minutes long. It shows the mistakes that the shopper made, e.g. signing up for an in-store contest and providing all of her personal information. All for some simple contest! The video has been seen by all of her friends and might even be used for a school project. What's important here was that, despite the video and advice being very simple, the bigger message was much more powerful.

Visit
www.BankruptAtBirthBook.com
to watch
Emily's two-minute-video.

When kids start to educate other kids about the risks of sharing their personal information, it gives us hope. This chapter provides more thoughts on the topic of identity theft and the role that we parents should play.

Well, the time you need to sit down with your kids and have the talk has finally arrived. No, not that talk. This is the one where you talk to them about online, social media, and mobile device safety. Whether your child is a pre-schooler or a high schooler, your goal should be the same. Obviously, the content of the conversation will be very different at different ages, but the goal should be to enlist them into a partnership to ensure their safety in this technological world.

By now, you have seen what can happen to kids whose identities are stolen. There should be no doubt that kids can endanger themselves as they text and tweet and visit social media websites. Whether your child is eight or 13, they need to understand that they are vulnerable to dangers out there, that we parents want them to remain safe.

As our kids get older, they have a greater stake in their own privacy. As parents, we have to respect their growing need for independence. Hopefully, we can find an acceptable line between a level of monitoring that leaves us comfortable yet doesn't overly impinge on their desire for independence and privacy. This line will shift as they grow and mature, and this line is not the same for all parents and kids. I can't tell you where to draw this line. What I can do is give you some thoughts on how to balance your need to protect them against their desire for privacy.

More and more these days, young kids are being given access to a computer in the home as a primary entertainment device. It is not too early for parents to sit down with a pre-schooler to discuss their use of a computer. At this early age, it's about parents setting limits. Parents should ensure that all parental controls are set on computers or devices their young children will use. They should go online with their children to find websites that are engaging and appropriate for their ages. This is not all that different from choosing what channels and programs a child can watch on television and for how long.

With young children, a parent or trusted older sibling should be with the child whenever they go onto the computer—at least to the point of getting them started—and do this each and every time. Then the parent, caregiver, or sibling should remain close by and check in frequently to see if the child needs help or encounters something risky.

For example, does your child know what to do if something suddenly pops up on the computer? Make sure they know to immediately ask you and not to click on anything or respond to anything. When in doubt, encourage them to ask you.

With younger children—and remember we are still talking about pre-schoolers—parents need to ascertain if their children have access to and are using computers outside the house. This usually occurs when they are at friends' houses. Ask your child if they are going onto computers at friends' houses, and if the answer is yes, inquire further to what kinds of activities they are engaging in, what kinds of games they are playing, and what websites they are visiting. If there is any doubt, confer with the other parent. This is no different from your child watching television at another house. What are they watching—is it appropriate? If they are on a computer—is it appropriate?

As your kids get older, their use of the computer will change. They may begin, or want to begin, socializing online. Now it's time to talk to them about online behavior, safety, and security, and to reach some understanding about and how, not whether, you will monitor their computer activities.

It's been our experience that children before or just entering their tween years are really looking for guidance rather than ways around supervision. At this point, your conversation with them about the Internet should focus first on the dangers that are out there. Talk about child identity theft, how it happens, and how they might inadvertently contribute to their own danger by what they post online. Talk about other online dangers and enlist their help in keeping themselves safe. Approach all of these discussions in a positive manner, stressing that you are working with them to have a full but safe Internet and social media experience.

Think about it this way: Focus on four Cs and one L: Conduct (theirs), Consequences, Content, Contacts, and Limits.

CONDUCT AND CONSEQUENCES

It's important that younger kids understand that their conduct online can have substantial consequences. What they say and what they post can come back to haunt them in the future. Impress upon them that what they think they are saying in private may not stay that way for long so to think twice before posting anything they wouldn't want to see going public. A thoughtless posting can ruin a friendship. Remind them that their reputations are at stake in what they say and what they post or forward online.

CONTENT

Many websites and online games are the equivalent of an R-rated movie that might expose them to a whole range of adult subject matter.

CONTACT

As your children get older, they will begin to roam more widely on the Internet. Inevitably, they will run across more adult or even very adult sites and images, often with very innocent-sounding names. If you can maintain an open relationship with your kids about the Internet, they should be able to come to you with questions about what they are finding. These are teachable moments.

With younger children, monitoring them, or limiting their abilities to visit certain areas of the Internet—or even more restrictive measures—should not be an area of contention. In fact, younger children should welcome your involvement and your interest in helping them. To most 12 or 13-year-olds who have a Facebook page, one absolute rule should be that they friend you. Another rule we recommend is that you get their password. These are not excessive requests. Likewise, limits on the amount of time they can spend online is likely not to be seen as unreasonable.

The tween years are the time you want to talk with your kids about bullying. By the time they reach middle school, they surely have explored the subject in some detail and have been warned against bullying others and to immediately let a teacher or counselor know if they have been bullied. You have probably encouraged them to talk to you about you about any incidents they see inside or outside of school.

Similarly, they should already know what is unacceptable computer and social media behavior. But now is the time to reinforce all aspects of the subject. It is important to point out that what, to them, might seem wholly innocent may be seen by the recipient or by the person the comment is about in a completely different light.

We have all seen these tragic stories about young people taking their own lives after being the subject of Internet bullying. A common thread in these stories is that the person doing the harassing did it unintentionally. They were simply making innocent fun or gossiping and are stunned by the consequences.

Mothers have said for generations, "If you don't have something nice to say about a person, don't say it." It may be a cliché, but it's one worth reminding our children about, especially in this new cyber world.

It is important to grant them more online responsibility as they become more experienced and as they mature, provided, of course, that they have shown they are ready for it. But you should make it clear that you are there to help any time, and they should not be afraid or embarrassed to ask for your help.

You will probably find that the welcoming of parental involvement in their online life is inversely proportional to the age of your children. Simply put, to teenagers privacy becomes of prime importance and parental monitoring becomes a flash point. As I noted in the previous chapter's discussion of monitoring, your request to have your child's Facebook password and to be friended, which was perfectly reasonable to a 12-year-old, is a declaration of war to a 16-year-old.

So how do you talk with that 16-year-old about online life and responsibilities? Hopefully, over a number of years, you have developed an open environment and an ongoing dialogue about online life and social media use. You have probably already had numerous talks about the implications attached to online behavior. Now is a good time to reinforce what you have been saying in the past—that what you say and what you post is probably there forever. Your child needs to be told again that what might seem innocuous at the time can damage their own reputations, endanger friendships, or even effect their own futures—colleges they will be applying to and employers they will be interviewing with even years from now will probably Google them and what has been posted now can lurk only to come forth and injure their future prospects.

SEXTING

Now is the time to bring up the subject of sexting—the sending of suggestive images of oneself to someone else. In 2009, the Pew Foundation, as part of its Internet & American Life Project, questioned teens on the subject. Pew researchers found that "four percent of cell-owning teenagers ages 12 to 17 say they have sent sexually suggestive nude or nearly nude images of themselves to someone else via text messaging and 15 percent of cell-owning teens ages 12 to 17 say they have received sexually suggestive nude or nearly nude images of someone they know via text messaging on their cell phone."[1]

Many young people think sexting is no big deal. The problem is that authorities think it is a big deal. Many state legislatures are passing laws criminalizing the act even when the photos are sent by the person in the photos. The big problem arises when the person depicted is under age 18. Ask a young man in Florida who has received sexted (and now it is a verb "to sext") images of his then girlfriend and who, after being "dumped" by her emailed the photos to all their friends and publicly posted them. He was arrested, prosecuted and, while sentenced to probation, now has to register as a sex offender for the next 25 years when he will be 43. He has been kicked out of college. He must ask his probation officer if he wants to travel outside the county. And, when he applies for a job, it is as a convicted felon.

The simple fact is a picture, as with any email or texted message, may be intended only for the recipient. But once you hit that send button, it's out there and you have lost control of it. At best, reputations can be lost; at worst, think of the young man in Florida.

MONITORING OLDER TEENS

With older teens, the flashpoint will be monitoring. What was completely acceptable to the 13-year-old will suddenly be seen as prying or worse to the 16-year-old. Much will likely depend on past acts. If they have done nothing in the past—save perhaps a few minor transgressions, you will have to loosen the leash and allow them greater Internet freedom.[2] Constant reminders of the dangers that lurk around the corners are in order. Kids making their own mistakes, in life as well as in their cyber lives, are part of growing up. Do what you've always done, and simply do your best to keep them safe.

SOFTWARE FOR MONITORING

In the previous chapter, I talked about the growing library of software that is becoming available to monitor or control your children's use of a smartphone. The same is available to use on their computers. With any of these software options, you can determine where on the Internet your children visit, who they talk with, and you can see what they say or are being told while being able to set limits on their access to certain sites or areas of the Web.

A common piece of advice that I often see on websites dedicated to telling you how to parent your kids online is that kids who have grown up using the computer and the Internet will be able to find workarounds to whatever controls you try to place on their computers, or smartphones, for that matter. The writers of this new generation of monitoring or access-limiting software say they are making this harder and harder for the average young person who is not themselves an advanced programmer or hacker.

One way kids have worked around having their parents monitor their Facebook page is by friending them and giving them their password, but then establishing a new gmail account under an alias and creating a second Facebook page using that alias—one that your parents are unaware of. The kids' friends know about the second page and that is where all the juicy stuff is placed—safe from prying parental eyes.

This sounds like a lot of work and no small measure of trickery. I believe that what parents should strive for is to develop an open, honest, and ongoing dialogue with their kids about their participation in the cyber-world. If this starts when the kids first begin wanting to use a computer and continues as they move into notebooks, netbooks, and smartphones this will be less of a wrenching experience for all involved. It's critical that your kids understand what you are trying to do is keep them safe and that you will give them more freedom as they grow older and more adept at using the technology and as they show they have earned that trust. This does not have to be an adversarial process.

Dutch security software developer AVG is conducting a global, multi-year, "Digital Diaries" research project aimed at determining how the Internet is impacting children as they play, learn, and grow up in today's digital world. Its latest version entitled "Digital Coming of Age," the latest phase of the study surveyed 4,400 parents with 14- to 17-year-olds in 11 countries.

The survey shows that 75 percent of American parents stay connected to their children via social networks, a much higher percentage than in other countries (the low is 10 percent in Japan). The survey reveals that 61 percent of American parents admitted accessing their kid's Facebook accounts without their knowledge, with mothers the most guilty.

In California, a bill being debated would force social networks like Facebook to allow parents access to their child's account(s) and force all privacy settings to their maximum level by default. Parents could also request images or text be removed from any social network page "upon request . . . within 48 hours." Any social network failing to conform would suffer a $10,000 fine per incident. Facebook is vigorously opposing the proposed law.[3]

So far we have discussed ways parents can minimize the exposure of their kid's SSN and we have discussed how parents can educate their kids to minimize the exposure of other information which could lead a criminal to discover their kid's SSN. In the next chapter we'll summarize that advice and give you a few more tips for protecting your kids from this crime. It's important to note, any person or service that promises to prevent identity theft—for adults or kids—is lying. Right now, as of today, there is absolutely no way to lock down your SSN and completely prevent identity theft—just like there is no way to prevent a home invasion—but there are things you can do to minimize the risk.

CHAPTER NINE:

THE PROBLEM WITH MOST CHILD ID THEFT ADVICE

My passion is identity theft education and protection, especially protecting the identities of children. I have learned that protecting your kids in this cyber-world is neither simple nor intuitive. It is a much more complex issue than I ever imagined, even as someone who does this for a living.

For a few years, we've been working on creating a new, patented service to protect children's identities. When we started thinking about and developing it we thought how hard can it be? Well, it turns there are many layers to this particular onion. We went into the project thinking we would be finished in about 90 days. Two years was closer to what we needed before we had something we were satisfied with.

Rather than just release something quickly, we built something that goes deep. I don't want to brag, but I'm really proud of what we've built. There is no other product on the market that can spot synthetic ID theft for kids.

In the last two years, I've learned a lot why most of the advice you get about child ID theft—from the government, the media, and yes, even our competitors in business, is way too simplified and ineffective. In this chapter, I'll share with you what I have learned. I bet you will be as surprised about some of this as I was.

Absolutely everywhere these days, from the experts at the Federal Trade Commission to every blogger to every media report, we are being given advice on how to keep our children safe from identity theft. What we are told, over and over, is that as concerned parents, we should check yearly, perhaps starting as early as our children's seventh birthday, whether our kids have credit reports on file with any of the three credit bureaus—Experian, TransUnion, and Equifax.

This is typical of the advice: The two best ways to protect your children from child identity theft are to either monitor your children's credit reports by obtaining a free credit report at least once a year or placing a credit freeze on your children's credit files if you reside in a state where that is permissible.

If the answer comes back "no record," we are told we can breathe a sigh of relief. Our child is safe. Just repeat this process yearly, or every couple of years, and we will be able to ensure when our kids need credit—because they are applying for a job, an apartment, some grant or student financial aid—there will be no stumbling blocks.

The advice of checking to see whether your child has an established credit file, when none should be in existence, is not so much completely wrong as it is alarmingly, and glaringly, incomplete. To start, and I can't be more emphatic on this point, the fact that one or even all three credit agencies come back with "no file" reports does not mean that your child's identity or personal information has not been stolen or compromised. To believe so is simply to misunderstand how the credit bureaus operate, what information they have or don't have, and what they can tell you at any given time.

Even people you would think are experts on the subject get it wrong. An example: The Texas State Comptroller's office revealed it had left the Social Security information of 3.5 million state workers online on an unsecured webpage. Whoops. So the comptroller's office offered those affected one year of free credit monitoring. That free year has run out so a spokesman for the Austin office of the Better Business Bureau, suggested any concerned workers take advantage of the mandated annual free credit reports from the big three reporting companies, but space the reports out over the course of the year "to better monitor your credit over the year."[1]

That advice assumes that, at any point in time, all three credit reporting bureaus possess the same information and, by getting a copy of one bureau's report, you know what all three have in their files. Wrong. Each bureau has different credit granters reporting to them so the information they have on an individual is often different from bureau to bureau. Larger creditors almost always report to all three, but the smaller granters of credit and the regional retailers and chains sometimes only report to a single bureau. Inquiries to the credit bureaus as to the credit worthiness of an individual and a request for a full report are also important because they are reflected in a credit file as activity, and if some granter of credit is asking for your file you want to know why. However, not all granters of credit get reports from all three bureaus. Only mortgage companies are required to use all three bureaus.

Theoretically, the three bureaus combine their files every so often, but that can be a hit-or-miss proposition and, at any one time, the files can differ significantly. It often takes 30 days after information is received by a bureau to be reflected in a specific file. If you are only receiving one report a year from only one of the three bureaus your identity may already have been compromised, and you won't see any indication for a considerable period after it has happened.

But to return to our central topic: determining whether your kids' identities or personal information has been stolen.

It's possible, although highly unusual, that someone has stolen both your child's name and Social Security number and established a phony persona using both. It happens certainly, but not with any great frequency. So even if the credit reports were complete, they would only be covering this tiny slice of identity theft.

Let's go back to our discussion of "synthetic" identity theft from chapter one. Synthetic ID theft is when a child's Social Security number is used in combination with another name—quite often the scammer's own name. It is this type of identity theft that is much more common—in fact, is the norm!

As far as the credit reporting agencies are concerned, an "identity" is composed of three elements: name, date-of-birth, and Social Security number. Of these, the least important is date-of-birth.

So if you try to ascertain if your children have credit files, ones possibly showing purchases they never made (not too many seven-year-olds buy houses, cars, or boats)or have open delinquent charge accounts) you will supply the child's name and Social Security number to be checked. The likely result will be, "no record" or "no file," unless someone has stolen both your child's Social Security number and their name. If only the Social Security number has been stolen and is being used, this check has essentially told you nothing.

Back to the data presented to the Federal Trade Commission at its Child Identity Theft Symposium last summer. Going in, the investigators knew that among the 42,000 children whose records were being checked against credit bureau files, there were 381 documented cases of identity theft. Despite the fact that it was eventually confirmed that fraudulent accounts in the credit bureau's files were linked to the stolen Social Security numbers in these cases, the initial credit bureaus review processes found only four of the already confirmed cases—a one-percent success rate. The other 99 percent returned a "no file found" when using the combination of both the child's actual name and the Social Security number.

This all traces back to how the credit bureaus check their files. They check the combination of name and Social Security number, usually not separate checks of names and Social Security numbers. The initial checking is done electronically. The response is instant, and thus so often is incomplete and misleading. In medicine, they would call it a false negative.

When we began work on our child identity theft protection program, KID SURE[SM], a number of the people involved in the product development effort who had children in the vulnerable age range checked to see if their own children might be having a problem. They utilized our own proprietary method rather than going directly to the three credit bureaus. All the reports came back negative, saying there were no records indicating the misuse of any of their children's Social Security numbers—except one. That one belonged to a colleague. We'll just call him Jeff. What Jeff has gone through to get to the bottom of what was happening to his son's identity is quite illuminating. He shares his story here:

"I checked my son's name and Social Security number through our own system, and it came back indicating there was a problem. Our system checks the records of the three credit bureaus and quite a bit more, and the report I got back indicated that something was amiss. Subsequently, digging deeper using our system, I learned that not one but two individuals were using my son's Social Security number, and one of them was actually using my son's name. This has apparently been going on for two-to-six years. They used my son's information to establish credit cards and store accounts. My son is only seven.

Armed with this information I went to two of three credit bureaus. In both cases, I talked directly with individuals. In both cases, they came back to me saying there were no problems.

Now I knew there were problems, and more than that I knew what the problems were. So we have been going back and forth with their dispute people trying to resolve the issues and clean up my son's records. I have not even gone to the third bureau yet, but I assume I will find the same thing.

If I had not been experienced with child identity theft problems, and if I had come in with no foreknowledge, I'm sure I would have gotten an all clear from both the bureaus. I would never have known my son has a problem."

It's important to stress once again that Jeff is an identity theft professional. He works continually with the credit bureaus investigating and resolving cases of identity theft. He knows what to ask, who to ask, and how to ask it. But had he been satisfied with the initial report of no file from the bureaus, he would have been relieved that his son's identity had not been compromised. However, from experience, he knew enough to persevere, to talk with a live person at each of the bureaus, and request a manual check for his son's Social Security number. Then, and only then, did he learn that his worst fears were realized.

It's also important to understand what information is in the files of the three credit reporting agencies and what information is likely not in there.

Imagine for the moment that you learn that the database at your health insurance company or maybe at your doctor's office or at your children's school has been hacked. You immediately become concerned that your children's personal data has been stolen and might already be in use by scammers. So you follow the advice you have been given and you check to see if any of the credit bureaus have a file under your child's name and Social Security number. It comes up negative. We've already seen why that is not just possible but likely in the case of synthetic identity theft. But even if someone has stolen both your child's name and Social Security number, here are more reasons why a "no file" response should not put your mind at ease.

Let's say that the database that contained your children's information was breached by a professional hacker, either alone or as part of a gang. Your child's name, Social Security number and other data has been put up for sale on the black market and is now in the hands of a scammer. That scammer uses it to obtain a cell phone, then rents an apartment, and has the utilities turned on all in your child's name—or in their own—using your child's Social Security number.

In the meantime, you are checking with the credit bureaus. You checked immediately after learning of the possibility that your child's ID might be in play. Now, maybe a year's time after getting an initial negative report—just to be safe—you check back a second time. By now, the scammer has walked away from a year's worth of rent, utility bills, and cell phone bills, and will do it again in some other kid's name. But you get back another "no record" report. How is this possible?

Let me give you another related scenario. Quite often these days I see reports that a company or a governmental agency had a data breach which exposed numerous people's confidential information. Typically the database owner notified everyone whose identities might have been compromised, apologized, guaranteed that their database was now definitely hacker proof and offered a year of free credit monitoring for anyone who was concerned. Now, a year later, the database owner reports that no one who took them up on their offer of credit monitoring has seen anything negative from the breach. So, says the database owner, it would appear everyone is out of the woods.

Maybe, but again, maybe not.

We tend to think of the credit reporting agencies as omnipotent. You would just assume that the three instances we spoke of: obtaining a cell phone, renting an apartment, and starting utilities would result in a credit file with multiple entries and now a record of delinquent accounts. Not necessarily. Not all transactions are reported to the credit bureaus. It is possible that none of the transactions described—apartment rental, utilities, and a cell phone were ever reported.

Apartment managers, cell companies, and utilities may not report accounts, even delinquencies. Many might have made an initial inquiry to any of the three credit bureaus. When the report of "no file" came back from the credit bureaus, the scammer would have had an excuse—a name change due to a divorce, etc.

The credit bureaus in reporting back "no record" may actually have started a temporary file under the name and Social Security number. But when after a certain period no further data is reported (remember realtors, cell phone companies, and utilities are not necessarily reporting), the "temporary" file may simply be discarded.

Or, there is another possibility. After the data breach exposing your child's information, their Social Security number was sold to an undocumented worker seeking employment. Using your child's Social Security number, the worker was able to be employed. A few months later that worker was cash-strapped so he went to a payday loan store and got a loan. Unable to pay it back or simply not wanting to pay it back, the undocumented worker who is now using your kid's Social Security number simply moved on. Was any of this reported to a credit bureau? Most likely not. So as far as checking the credit bureaus go, you would think there have been no negative repercussions from the data breach.

In many of these situations, what the credit bureaus don't know can come back to haunt your children because it's impossible to determine what will turn up when one of these previously unreported accounts or transactions comes into collection, and then the collection agency report it to the credit bureaus.

Of course, you or your child might just be the victim of bad timing. Often scammers are not using a particular false identity for any significant length of time. They open a charge account, possibly make one payment after a small purchase, and then use that account to acquire another. They attempt to max them both out and move on to the next false identity. This process is called "burning and churning."

You may have learned that your child's personal data has been exposed, possibly through a breach. So you immediately check with the credit bureaus as you have been advised and the reports comeback no record. You breathe a sigh of relief.

A year or two later, you check again. Or even worse, your child applies for credit. Now you find there is a credit file showing the open and long past due account or accounts. You're stunned. The files show the accounts were opened before you checked previously. What happened?

It takes time, perhaps as long as 90 days for information to travel from a credit granter to the credit bureau and for a file to be established. A check in that interim period will most often be returned as no file. In this case, you moved too quickly.

No state has had as many problems with data breaches and unintended exposure of private information as the State of Utah, and no state has taken as proactive an approach to fighting the effects of identity theft as Utah. Utah Assistant Attorney General, Richard Hamp, was hired in 2000 specifically to prosecute cases under Utah's aggressive ID theft statute.

He immediately began to uncover problems. First, he discovered a mortgage fraud scheme that used stolen Social Security numbers, many of which belonged to children in the state. Then he uncovered an unusually high incidence of the theft of identities of children in foster homes or other state-sponsored social programs.

"In our state, Workforce Services maintains two data sets," Hemp related to the Federal Trade Commission symposium last summer. "One is everybody who is employed in the state, or unemployed in the state. (Another) keeps track of people who are on some sort of public-assistance program. So if your child is receiving public assistance in Utah, it's in the same data sets that Workforce Services has. So this gives Workforce Services the unique ability to say, "Okay, I've got a kid here receiving public assistance who's six years old, but that kid is also reflected as a brick mason making $30,000 a year." And I have prosecuted a number of those cases at this stage and can tell you—I've got kids that are brick masons. I've got kids that are waitresses. I've got kids that are carpenters. And some of them are making better wages than what I am making." He knew these were obvious incidents of child identity theft.[2]

If you think that your identity has been stolen, or even jeopardized because your personal information is contained in a database that has been hacked or compromised, one thing you can do if you are an adult with an established credit history and thus have active files with the credit-reporting agencies, is request the three major credit reporting companies to put a "freeze" on your file. By locking access to your credit file, it will mean a granter of credit cannot check your credit, and they will not open a new account for someone trying to use your stolen data.

Previously, the credit bureaus would put a freeze on your file only if you could make a showing that identity theft had already occurred, not just that you are a prospective victim. It costs these agencies money because they are not able to supply credit reports to their clients, as well as the cost involved in implementing such as system. They resisted and, as a result, 48 states have now passed statutes requiring the credit reporting agencies to institute freezes upon request.

Hemp was the author of Utah's law requiring freezes upon request and, as he told the Identity Theft Symposium, when a state legislator came to him as asked if he would draft a similar statute aimed at protecting children, he said, "I thought, wow, that sounds easy enough. I went back to my credit freeze statute, figured I could alter about one line and make it a child credit freeze statute and drafted up a bill."

Nope, not so fast, as Hemp soon found out. He leaned that this would only work "if the kid has already been compromised and has a credit file open. I said, "Really? I kind of want to prevent it up front, rather than waiting until after. Why doesn't that work?"

So he took that question to TransUnion and got a simple answer: "We can't freeze something that doesn't exist yet."

So as Hemp related, " I said . . . we need to solve this problem. I have got thousands of kids in my state that have been compromised, and I want do something to protect them, but apparently, the process doesn't exist." So basically TransUnion has worked with the State of Utah to come up with a process that is called the Utah Attorney General's Child Identity Protection (CIP) program.

> "We've created a portal on our IRS website where parents can come in and register their kids," Hemp related. "We will check the parents' information through a verification system that exists already in Utah for voter registration online. We will then feed that information to TransUnion, along with the kid's information, with the fact that we've at least verified the parents' information. TransUnion then will have the ability to take the child's name and number and put it on their high-

risk fraud alert. So if someone's attempting to open credit in that kid's name, there will is a message pinged back from TransUnion saying, "Check further. There may be a problem."

Technically, what is happening is TransUnion is establishing a credit file for these whose information is coming in from Utah, and then putting a freeze on that empty file.

Hemp says he gets inquiries from other states wanting to duplicate this program. But he correctly notes that TransUnion is only one of three bureaus providing credit reports, and that essentially you are asking them to change their basic business model from issuing credit reports for which they charge their customers, to not issuing credit reports.

In its most recent session, the Maryland State Legislature passed the Child Identity Lock Bill, which its chief sponsor, Delegate Craig Zucker, says he hopes will serve as a national model.[3]

The bill, as introduced, was fairly straightforward. It said a parent or legal guardian could request on the part of a "protected consumer"—by definition a child under the age of 16 or an incapacitated person—a freeze be put on their credit report. The key section of the proposed new law as introduced said:

> "If a consumer for whom a security freeze is requested by the consumer's representative does not have a consumer report at the time of the request, the consumer reporting agency shall create a consumer report for the consumer for the purpose of imposing a security freeze on it in accordance with this section."

That is clear and very straightforward. But then the lobbyists, the credit bureaus, big credit granters and the like began to weigh in and, by the time the new law made it to final passage, the very clear-cut definitions and the requirement to create a credit file for a child and then freeze it upon request, got a bit obfuscated and was turned into this:

> "Record means a compilation of information that identifies a protected consumer; is created by a consumer-reporting agency solely for the purpose of complying with this section;

and may not be created or used to consider the protected consumer's creditworthiness, credit standing, credit capacity, character, general reputation, personal characteristics or mode of living."

So a credit file would not be created, rather "a compilation of information." It would exist solely to be frozen, which is not unlike Utah's arrangement with TransUnion. But it could not be used like a credit file for any of the purposes for which a credit file exists. Then too, the definition of a consumer's representative becomes a bit confusing as does the powers of that representative.

"One of my proudest accomplishments as a delegate was passing the Child Identity Lock Bill, which gives parents a tool to protect their children from identity theft," Zucker said. "With this legislation, parents will be able to freeze their child's credit, completely preventing the child's personal information from being used fraudulently. Child identity theft is a growing problem in the United States, but my hope is that the Child Identity Lock bill helps parents stop fraud before it affects their kids."

"This goes into effect on January 1, 2013. Once it is in effect, you will simply need to contact one of the major credit rating agencies (Experian, TransUnion or Equifax) and provide them with the requested information to freeze your child's credit."[4]

It is still too early to tell how effective the Maryland law is going to be or how effective the Utah program is going to be. Possibly it will have an effect and will offer some measure of protection and peace of mind for worried parents. Maybe it will, but probably not.

As a starting point, a call to one credit bureau does not encompass all three. You will have to contact all three and follow procedures not yet in existence. It's also not clear exactly where and how these compilations of information will be stored on each of the credit bureau's systems or, most importantly, how they will be searched. Will they result in a hit if just the Social Security number is being used? Or will they only ping back if the combination of name and Social Security number is being scammed? That is left unclear.

But the positive thing about the new Maryland law (and it only covers citizens of the State of Maryland) is that it shows the problem of child identity theft has begun to percolate up into the consciousness of the politicians. The new Maryland law can serve as a model, albeit if other states write their laws in a broader and much more straightforward way.

So you can see the universally given "just order a credit report" is incomplete, and even the more forward-thinking attempts to thwart child identity theft such as the Utah/TransUnion model, and the new Maryland law, can really only bring parents limited peace of mind.

This seems a good point to interject a pair of identity theft stories that are both extreme in nature—one a story of adult identity theft one a story of child identity theft. The first is thanks to Steve Mayes and published in his column in the Portland Oregonian newspaper.

Kimberly Fossen was said not to be a nice person. That's at least what the NYPD believed. The NYPD believed she would lure unsuspecting men, drug them, and steal everything. In October 2009, Fossen accompanied a 38-year-old man to his Queens apartment, drugged him and, when he finally came to, she had disappeared along with his Rolex watch, gold rings, passport, Louis Vuitton bag, and Jeep Cherokee.[5]

How did they know the culprit was Kimberly Fossen? They had a sample of her DNA from the Queens apartment, and it matched samples taken from a woman identified as Fossen when she was arrested for similar crimes in Florida and Nevada.

Now here she was, apparently living in the Portland suburb. New York detectives asked the Clackamas County (Oregon) Sheriff's Office to locate Fossen. They did and sent a copy of Fossen's driver's license photo to New York. "The picture looks like the same girl I am searching for," an NYPD detective told the Oregon Sheriff's office.

On Nov. 4, 2009, Clackamas County deputies, accompanied by New York cops, arrested Fossen at her home. She was jailed, hauled before a judge, and held for extradition to New York.

But there was a problem. Her fingerprints did not match those taken from the crime scene in New York or those on record in Nevada. Whoops, said the cops, as they released her.

A year earlier, a Clackamas County deputy had told Fossen a woman arrested in Las Vegas had a Florida driver's license issued in her name. She knew she was the victim of identity theft and tried to tell the arresting officers to check her fingerprints or DNA before she was arrested. Instead, she spent a day in jail before the identity theft was confirmed and she was released.

"It was horrific," Fossen told a Portland television station. She had been searched, given jail garb, and put in a holding cell with other inmates. The worst part, she said, was being paraded in chains before her daughter. "I wanted to die," Fossen said.

> "There's nothing you can do," Fossen said in a KATU interview. "You're totally helpless. Nothing you can say matters. It's a very traumatizing ordeal."[6]

Eventually, the New York cops got the right woman: Minh Thuy Nguyen, 23, from Norcross, Georgia. Nguyen pleaded guilty to second degree grand larceny and was sentenced to five years probation.

It's not clear how Nguyen and Fossen crossed paths. Fossen's purse was stolen in 2000 and again in 2004. She did not file police reports but did check her credit reports for fraudulent activity. She saw nothing unusual.

Nguyen had done it before. She also posed as Lien Thi Huynh, 26, also of Norcross, Georgia, a former high school classmate. Nguyen moved to Florida, assumed Huynh's identity, and soon was convicted of prostitution and other crimes. "I started getting (notices of) court dates coming to my home," Huynh said. "I've never been arrested in my life."

From that point on, police and court records listed Huynh as a criminal. Nguyen escaped detection. Soon, Fossen became another of her victims.

This is a case of adult identity theft. But what happened one night in Southern California tells much the same story.

Members of a federal warrant taskforce came knocking on a door, and a woman who had been watching television answered. We have an arrest warrant for an individual we believe is living here, they announced. Yes, she told them, he does live here. I'll get him. A few minutes later, she emerged with her five-year-old son wiping the sleep from his eyes. He was in his jammies.

It was another case of identity theft. It would be almost amusing if it were not for the fact that the Task Force members were not all that surprised. This identical thing was happening with appalling regularity.

Our point in relating these two stories is to show that a parent concerned about identity theft should not simply stop at quizzing the three credit bureaus. The credit bureaus don't check court records or arrest records. As I've pointed out, most credit reporting agencies do not receive records of cell phone accounts being established, or apartments being rented or utility accounts being started. Nor do they receive information about payday loans or employment for that matter.

Actually the Social Security Administration will allow a parent to ascertain if their child's Social Security number is being used for employment. You need to go down to your nearest Social Security office in person, bring your child's birth certificate, Social Security card, proof of parenthood or guardianship, and then fill out some forms so you can learn if someone, somewhere, is using your child's Social Security number.

TO GET THE PEACE OF MIND YOU ARE ENTITLED TO:

» Monitor the Internet for your child's Social Security number and other data.

» Monitor public record data by looking for matches for the child's name, Social Security number, date of birth, and address.

» Monitor the Internet and other sources for new accounts, loans, cell phones, etc., using the child's name, Social Security number, or date of birth.

Then, even if you are able to dedicate yourself to this degree, you always have the problem of what the medical profession calls "false positives." Maybe your child's Social Security number shows up in a distant court filing. Is it a case of their identity having been stolen, or is it simply a case of a harried court employee typing in a wrong number that, by coincidence, is the same as your child's? Regretfully, such errors happen all too often.

The simple answer to all this is you personally can't be vigilant to this degree. Even if you had the determination and the hours to do so, you simply don't have the technology. Therefore, you need to find a service that does, and several of them do exist.

Is the problem of child identity theft insolvable, one that is simply destined to grow and grow exponentially, and dependent on concerned parents to head it off for their own children on a case-by-case basis? Hopefully not, but to really begin to make headway against the growing tide, it is going to take the active cooperation of government, law enforcement, major entities in the private sector, and it's going to take time, money and, above all, collective will to see the problem of child identity theft eradicated.

Actually, a bill before Congress could go a long way toward putting a dent in child identity theft. H.R. 2885, the Legal Workforce Act, a bipartisan bill that was approved by the Judiciary Committee but never made it to the House floor requires the Social Security Administration to allow individuals to "lock" their own Social Security number, or those of their children, so they cannot be used by imposters to verify work eligibility. In addition, H.R. 2885 requires individuals who have likely been victims of identity theft for work authorization purposes to be notified of that likelihood so they can then take steps to prevent further illegal use of their identity.

This could go a couple steps further. It starts at the doorstep of the Social Security Administration. Every time a new Social Security number is issued to a minor, that number, along with the identity of the child to whom it is issued, is entered into a limited access database. This new database has to be secure, and it has to be made available both to law enforcement, the Internal Revenue Service and, most importantly, to the three major credit reporting agencies.

Every time the credit reporting agencies receive an inquiry, they have to run the Social Security number against this new Social Security Administration database of new numbers issued to minors. Obviously, if they have a five-year-old trying to buy a car or applying for a credit card, or if the IRS determines a child living in one state is apparently seeking a major tax refund from a distant state, it will be readily apparent that something is wrong and that fraud is evident. This would be promptly reported to whoever is making the credit inquiry and to the appropriate law enforcement entity.

Obviously, it is going to take time to develop and time to compile enough Social Security numbers for it to be effective both in exposing fraud and acting as a deterrent.

Such a plan could also allow parents to voluntarily add their children's Social Security numbers. This would increase its size exponentially and would require even more funding to administer and maintain. But, it would allow us to get to where we want to be more quickly.

Unfortunately, at a time when we have a government that cannot even establish a budget and agree on priorities, such an undertaking is clearly somewhere between wishful thinking and pure fantasy. In the meantime, parents like us are simply going to have to find a combination of means to keep our kids safe from identity theft.

In the next chapter, we'll talk about what to do if the worst happens and your child becomes a victim. Unwinding identity theft is never easy, but we've put together some advice that will help if this is a situation you find yourself in.

CHAPTER TEN:

A PARENTS' GUIDE TO CHILD ID THEFT RECOVERY

As I keep saying, our central purpose in writing this book is to help parents understand the danger child identity theft poses to their children and then how to best keep them safe. But sometimes, no matter how hard we try, it happens. Their identity is stolen.

It can be among a parent's worst nightmares. But once it has happened, how do you help your child recover their good names and their financial futures?

My colleagues and I deal with this every day, and we see how difficult recovery can be. We also see what happens when parents unknowingly allow this problem to fester. But recovery can be done, with enough knowledge and enough perseverance.

Hopefully, this chapter will never be needed by you, but we have learned through experience it might. Startlingly to us, when we were testing a product, several of our colleagues decided to make sure their own children's identities had not been compromised. To their surprise, and ours, one of their kid's identities had, in fact, been stolen. This really hit home.

Again, we hope you'll never need this, but if you do, please read the following very closely.

As you are about to see, recovering from identity theft, and from child identity theft in particular, is time consuming and at times amazingly frustrating. It can be expensive, even though what has occurred is through no fault of yours and certainly no fault of your child. Luckily, recovery is doable, but you must be disciplined and thorough.

Earlier, we saw several cases of child identity theft that haunted the victims for a very long time after the identity theft was discovered. What parents need to understand is that sometimes seemingly very simple cases of child identity theft, ones that you think are easily corrected, can have lasting repercussions. Just ask Lisa Garza of Texas.[1]

Ten years ago, turning 18, Lisa wanted to make sure she didn't have anything negative lurking in a credit file. Naturally she had a copy of her credit report pulled. To her surprise, listed on the report, were delinquent accounts with a utility company. The surprise was she had never opened such an account because, at the time, she was still living at home.

She and her mother sent an affidavit to the utility company saying that Garza had always lived at home and had never opened an account with the utility. The utility company removed the information from her "account" and notified the credit bureau. Case closed? Not quite. Her problems were just beginning.

A year or so later, she started looking for her first apartment. Her application was turned down because another credit report showed her delinquent in rent from an apartment complex she had never heard of. It took some effort, but this too was resolved. End of story? Nope.

It appears that the person or persons who stole Lisa's identity and Social Security number used the information in applying for more than one job. Those employers in due course sent in W-2 wage reports to the IRS listing "Lisa Garza" as the recipient of wages. Now her problems were really beginning.

When the real Lisa filed her tax returns, the IRS declined to issue an expected refund because its records showed she had income she had never claimed and thus owed back taxes. Lisa says she and her husband did not get an almost $6,000 refund they expected, money they needed for medical expenses.

So Lisa and her tax preparer wrote the IRS, trying to straighten out this mess. Remember, this was a full 10 years after she first learned someone was using her identity and Social Security number. Lisa was now 28 years old and pregnant, and the refund in question was in a joint return she filed with her husband.

> "My new husband and I are expecting our first child together, and since private insurance in Texas does not include maternity care, we must cover the expenses ourselves," she added. "This is especially difficult, since we are both students and the income we do receive covers our living expenses and not much else."

Things dragged on and it appeared that the IRS was turning a deaf ear to situation. It would not respond to Lisa's letters. Then columnist Pamela Yip wrote about Lisa's problem in the Dallas Morning News and things began to move.

It ended up that three different IRS Service Centers in different parts of the country had to go in and retroactively change tax returns and documents. It was not one year's taxes that were involved but multiple years and W-2s received in different parts of the country. Lisa received one check from the IRS, but one Service Center was still dunning her for $2,402 in back taxes for 2006.

"They're still claiming that I owe money, which baffled me because I made less than $400 that year," Garza said.

Lisa's case will eventually get resolved. The IRS is not the bad guy here because they are simply inundated with such cases each of which can take many hours to straighten out. But Lisa's case shows how what might be thought of as a relatively simple case of child identity theft—a utility bill and an apartment lease—can turn into more than a decade of turmoil.

One of the oddest cases I have seen is that of Ann, whose long battle trying to erase the stain of identity theft, is hopefully now over, but she doesn't know for sure. Ann tells her story:

In 1998, a woman living in the New York City area opened at least 22 accounts using her name and address, and my Social Security number. Most of the accounts were for bank-issued credit cards, a few were for department store credit cards, and one was for a health club membership. She would use the cards for a while and run up a balance and then stop making any payments. Most of the cards had a balance of under $1,000.

In 2002, my husband and I met with a mortgage broker to refinance the house that we purchased in 1997. When he ran my name and social, my accurate credit history came up. When he ran just my social, the credit history that came up on his computer was three times the size of my own. The mortgage broker helped me track down the city and state that the accounts originated from.

I filed a police report in NYC, and the woman was arrested. She was carrying quite a few of the cards at the time of her arrest. When I asked her where she got the Social Security number she used, she said she just made it up. Since it worked, she said she kept using it to obtain more accounts.

She fled before her trial. I never met her and have no idea who she is or where she is. She was not informed of my name or anything else about me.

I was running a design firm in 2002. I had the help of my bookkeeper who is also a notary and a CPA. I had all the computer equipment in the world and a fax machine and copy machine at my disposal. I also had the help of the mortgage broker. Clearing my credit history became my hobby. It was important to clear my name because the 10-person design firm I was running was relying heavily on personal guarantees for everything from our office lease to our payment terms with our vendors.

Over the next six months, I sent certified letters to all of the banks where she had opened an account. I referenced their account numbers. I sent a copy of my Social Security card and my driver's license and the police report number. Some of the places would call me, some would just respond through the mail. They would send me an affidavit to fill out. Each and every account was cleared off of my credit history. We refinanced the house as well.

Once everything was cleared and I had a clean report from all three credit agencies, I did not give it another thought. My husband and I bought another house in 2005 and had no problem with the mortgage application. My overall feeling about it was that it was an annoyance.

But, I had done nothing wrong, and the banks understood that it was not my debt. In fact, I was just as annoyed at the banks for not checking the accuracy of the information before they issued credit to the wrong person.

Problem solved, right? That was in 2005. For a full decade, Ann heard nothing. She assumed it was just a bad incident that she long ago had corrected and put behind her. Then round two began.

In January, 2012, I received an alert from my bank that I had insufficient funds in my checking account and another that I had insufficient funds in my savings account to cover a payment to someone for over $4,000. I called the bank, and they admitted that funds had been removed from my account, and they gave me a number to call. I called the number and they told me that this was an attempt to collect a debt. I told them that no one had contacted me about a debt. They asked for my name but could not find the case using my name. They asked for my husband's name but could not find it under his name. They asked for the docket number, but I did not have a docket number. They insisted that I give them my Social Security number. I refused.

I called the bank and got the docket number. Called the collection agency back but they could still not discuss the case with me because they did not have my name on file. I finally gave them my Social Security number to look up the case. That's when the collection agency rep asked me, "Who is Lou?" I told him I didn't know. When he said Lou Anthony, it all came back to me.

Palisades Collection, LLC, using their law firm Pressler and Pressler, had obtained a NY court order to put a lien on my bank accounts. They were attempting to collect a 10-year-old AT&T bill. That account never came up in the original fraud case. I did not know it was out there.

Bank of America had no alternative than to freeze my accounts. The court order said her name and then added my name as a AKA. This scared me more than I care to admit. It was bizarre and completely out of the blue. I filled out an Identity theft victim's complaint and affidavit that I found online, and I went to the bank the next morning. I brought my husband because both of the accounts are in both of our names. I was also so angry and upset, I could hardly think straight. We had no access to cash and no idea how to convince a collection agency that they had the wrong person.

We met with the branch manager for over two hours. I had the affidavit notarized and came to understand what had happened and why it appeared as though the bank had given away my money to someone I didn't even know. There was nothing the bank could do to help me other than freeze the account and not release the money. They did that because the court order was not addressed to me alone. I had also been with this bank since 1997. It took many phone calls to Pressler and Pressler.

It also took phone calls from the bank's branch manager. I also faxed all of the letters from all of the other banks that had cleared the fraud case 10 years ago. I even found the New York detective who had made the arrest back then. He remembered the case well. I begged Pressler and Pressler to call him.

They were in no rush to do anything. Remember, all our money was still tied up in a frozen account. I threatened them with a lawsuit. Things began to move quickly.

Finally, after days of dealing with this, Pressler and Pressler finally lifted the restraint and sent an order to vacate to Bank of America. They said they were sorry! The bank sent my money to me in a check and waved all of the charges involved with being overdrawn.

I am, of course, worried that somehow this whole nightmare will repeat itself in the future. Someone will sue me over a decades-old debt. So I went to the Federal Trade Commission site and filled out a fraud affidavit. I was told to file a report with the Fairfax County Police (where I now live). But I could not because no new crime had been committed. I got nowhere with any of the government institutions.

I learned that the crook's name is still on my information reports at the credit reporting services as someone using the same Social Security number. I'm still trying to get that removed. I also learned that when an old debt is sold to a collection agency, it should pop up at the credit- eporting services as a new transaction. So I have signed up with a good private service to continually monitor my credit reports and their other sources of information. It's helped a great deal with peace of mind, but I still worry.

There are several morals to this awful story. One is, as Yogi Berra reminded us, "It ain't over til it's over." In identity theft cases, you don't know what can still be lurking out there in some file that might come back to haunt you, and you have to do everything you can to minimize this possibility. You need to immediately clear your child's record and you need to be thorough to be sure the problem will not resurface in the future as it did for Lisa Garza or Ann. Then too, in Ann's case, she had voluminous files she kept over the years documenting everything, keeping every document, letter, affidavit, etc. When the problem hit 10 years later, she could just reach in this file.

So, what if you have determined—or suspect—that your child's identity has been stolen? The answer is a bit different depending on exactly what you have discovered and how you have discovered it.

Say, for instance, your child has gotten a letter from the Internal Revenue Service asking why a tax return has not been filed covering the income received from some employment. Or you may have received a call from a collection agency demanding payment on a delinquent account. Or, your child has been denied a student loan or admission because of a negative credit report.

Outrage aside, our first piece of advice is, above all, do not ignore it. Your child is six and a collection agency has called, and you have told them your six-year-old does not have a credit account at some store. You have to assume the call is just the tip of the iceberg, so to speak. Don't assume that one call will solve what might be a major problem. It may just be that your work has just begun.

Initially, you need to put an end to what has surfaced. You are going to have to gather a number of documents for each step of the way. You will need to put together a packet containing the following (and you might as well make multiple copies of every one because you could end up sending out many). The packet needs to contain:

» Your child's birth certificate listing parents

» Your child's Social Security card

» Your child's addresses for the last five years

» Your child's school records for the past five years

» Proof of your relationship to the child (which might be covered by the birth certificate or else adoption or guardian documents)

» Your government-issued identification card, such as a driver's license or military identification or copies of documents proving you are the child's legal guardian

» Proof of your address, like a utility bill, credit card, or insurance statement, ideally with a five-year history of residence

» In some states, and under some circumstances, you may need to obtain and file a Uniform Minor's Status Declaration

» A notarized statement that you are requesting information or acting on your child's behalf as the child's parent and legal guardian

» A statement that you are requesting documents based on fraud associated with your either your child's identity or Social Security number pursuant to FCRA 609(e).

This rather simple gathering of documents can get awfully complicated if the child has been adopted, or if there has been divorce, re-marriage, custody contest or the like. But now you understand what you are going to need.

With our example of a collection agency call you need to put the account into dispute, and find out the details of the debt. You need to determine if the fictitious account has been opened both in your child's name and Social Security number, or just the number now attached to a different name. You next need to contact the merchant, inform them that identity theft has occurred, and demand the account be closed and that fact communicated to the credit bureaus.

Don't be surprised if your seemingly simple request is met with some degree of skepticism. A growing major area of fraud is people with completely legitimate debts notifying the givers of credit and credit bureaus that they are the victims of identity theft and try to have the legitimate debts removed from their records.

So, you will need to convince the granter of credit that your child is a victim. Speak to the company's fraud department and provide whatever documents they require (most likely your document package) plus some other affidavits. Also make sure they are sent certified return receipt and add everything to your project file, which will grow much larger as you progress.

Now you have to find how big a problem you and your child face.

First, go to your local police and ask that a police report be filed. Remember, as in our collection call example, you know that identity theft has occurred. The police should file a report. Keep the copy. If you are in a situation where you believe identity theft might have occurred, the police might not be inclined to file a report.

Next, file a complaint with the Federal Trade Commission (https://www. ftccomplaintassistant.gov/). This might seem like a so-what kind of thing, but at certain points in the future, you can count on being asked if this has occurred. Make and keep a copy of your filing.

The Federal Trade Commission's Identity Theft Report is like a police report with more than the usual amount of detail. The Identity Theft Report includes enough detail about the crime for the credit reporting companies and the businesses involved to verify that you are a victim—and to know which accounts and inaccurate information came from identity theft. Normal police reports often don't have many details about the accounts that were opened or misused by identity thieves.

Now you need to contact the three credit bureaus and to repeat once again: TransUnion by email at childidtheft@transunion.com, and by phone Experian (1–888–397–3742) and Equifax (1–800–525–6285). Tell each you have proof of identity theft based on one account in your child's name being placed for collection, and ask each to perform a manual search first for your child's name and Social Security number combined and then a separate manual search for just their Social Security number. They will ask you to document your child's identity and your identity as the child's parent or guardian. So send a copy of your packet and also include a copy of the Federal Trade Commission's Identity Theft Report.

You need to demand the actual copies of what turns up. Again the consistent advice is to "freeze" your child's credit report and to put a fraud alert on it. But, once again, we come back to the fact you can't freeze what does not exist. Maybe, just maybe, someone has stolen your child's complete identity. There may be a credit report—with one or more of the reporting agencies— essentially in your child's name and with their Social Security number, but with a different address. Don't simply to freeze that report. You need to eliminate it, as it contains completely fraudulent information. And be sure that report is not sent out while you work on not just cleaning it up, but wiping it out. Finally, establish a correct report on your child, which might not have anything in it, but you can place a fraud alert on that new, correct report to ensure that no one tries to fraudulently establish credit.

All of what you are reporting is not going to sound strange to the fraud people at the three credit agencies. They are probably working on dozens upon dozens of similar cases. You just need to be polite and calm, and to work with them. But you need to be diligent and proactive, and stay in constant contact with them to ensure your case moves forward.

If accounts have been opened in the name of your child, you need to contact the merchant or merchants' fraud departments in writing, sending the notifications via return receipt, while keeping copies of everything, and expressing that fraud has occurred and asking that the accounts be closed and the closure for fraud be reported to all three credit reporting agencies.

Each merchant will have a different process. Stick with it. Only speak with fraud investigators when contacting credit issuers or collection agencies, not just traditional customer-service personnel. (Remember, your child is most likely a minor and can't legally enter into a contract so don't fall for any kind of collection tricks). Don't rest until all accounts have been closed and you have written acknowledgement that all have been closed, and that all have been closed because of fraud.

You should now be left with a credit report with none of the negative information caused by the identity thief. You now must monitor the report, at least annually, to make sure nothing erroneous has found its way onto the report. If it has, it must be dealt with aggressively and immediately. Ideally, you should get a monitoring service—and one that monitors not just the items on a credit report but for synthetic ID theft; that is, when a child's Social Security number is used with another name. There are several products on the market. Ours is KID SURE^{SM}, and we believe it is by far, the most complete of the available products. When monitoring just a credit report, you miss at least half of the evidence that may be out there, if not more.

If your child's problem is with the IRS, or you find their Social Security number has been used by someone else to gain employment, the fraud bureaus at both the IRS and the Social Security Administration must be contacted, and the process of each agency to clean the record must be started and completed. Again, what you are reporting will not seem unusual to them. In fact, they may be so deluged, that it will take some time to work your way through their processes.

We have kept our example fairly simple. One identity thief has opened some merchant accounts in your child's name and/or with your child's Social Security number and has either skipped payment (most likely) or is horribly delinquent. Or someone has used the Social Security number to gain employment or to receive medical treatment. Now, instead of one person committing fraud, think about if there were several people, or a half-dozen, or a dozen. Essentially, it is the same problem multiplied a number of times. It is essentially the same solution multiplied a number of times.

Your child's identity has been stolen. Likely the question will arise as to whether you need to hire a lawyer. The only answer we can give here is that depends on your individual circumstances. It may depend on who the identity thief is—a stranger or strangers, or whether it's a member of the family. If it is the latter, is the identity theft tied to an ongoing divorce or custody battle? If so, a family law specialist might need to be involved.

Is there litigation involved? Is your child being sued? If so a lawyer might be more effective in resolving the various issues. Is it a tax matter and if so, is it complicated? A tax lawyer may have to become involved. You have to be the judge of this.

We should mention that under some circumstances, the Social Security Administration will issue the victim of identity theft a new Social Security number. They are more willing to do so when the present number might be being used by multiple offenders and especially when the age of the victim is still quite young. In those circumstances, this is worth exploring.

Is all this easy? Heck, no. But it is essentially to ensure your child grows up with a clean identity, a clean credit history and, above all, does not find themselves in the situation faced by Ann or any of the other victims we have seen.

Finally, there are services, lawyers, and consultants who will do the monitoring, protecting, and recovering for you. At times, they may be more effective than you trying to do all this yourself—more effective because they deal with all the players every day, they know what needs to be done and how to do it, and they can probably get you better, faster results than you might be able to yourself. Now, you have the added burden of making sure you are dealing with a reputable individual or organization and that they are just as determined to get a completely positive outcome as you are.

Almost inevitably during this process, you will be asking yourself why me, why my child? There is no real answer. It's happened, so now you do what any parent has to do after any kind of accident, you deal with it. Fortunately (but regrettably), all this is happening to so many young people that the people, organizations, and services you will be dealing with have pretty much heard it all before. They will understand what you are going through and what is necessary to resolve your problem. You just have to remember that it helps to be proactive and to stay positive. There is light at the end of the tunnel, and hopefully your tunnel, if you have to enter one, will not be too long.

Visit
www.BankruptAtBirthBook.com
to subscribe to the
Child ID Theft News.

FINAL THOUGHTS

As you've discovered, there's no shortage of stories, statistics, and examples of identity theft in our lives. It is, once again, the number one crime reported to the Federal Trade Commission. And, with over nine million consumers affected each year, odds are very good that someone you personally know will be—or has been—a victim of identity theft. We hope that we've been able to help you reduce these odds (as well as give you guidance on what to do if you've become a victim).

We're also hopeful that you now understand the stark reality that identity thieves do not discriminate based on age. Thankfully, some of our state governments and federal agencies have begun to take notice—and take action. The challenge for all of us is that our information—and in many cases, the information of our children—is already out there...like toothpaste from a tube. It's impossible to put back.

The changing landscape of technology, social media, and consumer behavior—coupled with a troubled economy—has created very fertile ground for identity thieves. As a society, we are exposed. Add to this the fact that a child's identity has become more appealing than ever and what we're left with is a very bleak outlook. We can, however, be more aware of how thieves attempt to obtain and use our information and the information of our children. We need to take this personally. We need to change our behavior. We need to regain our sense of ownership. And, we need to explain what we mean when we say, "Don't talk to strangers" to our children. It's clear that such a statement has taken on a completely new meaning since our childhood.

Despite being in the business of protecting people's identities, we are both constantly amazed at the creativity of thieves and the ease in which information can be obtained and used against us. We are exposed simply by virtue of the world that we live in. The fact that we have become so vulnerable and that such thefts can occur should make all of us very angry. And while there's no magic bullet, there are steps that we can take to curb this problem.

Joe Mason
Chantilly VA
July 2012

AFTERWORD

When Joe suggested he write a book on identity theft, my first reaction was, "That's crazy! We're not authors or a publishing house; we are a product company just trying to help consumers understand the dangers of ID theft and how to protect themselves. "

Of course, that was the point.

As authors we'd have a platform to educate consumers about identity theft. Around the same time, we were learning more and more about a new, unscrupulous kind of ID theft—Child ID Theft. That's when I knew the time was right to claim our status as authors. We might be able to make a real difference to parents and kids who are largely unaware of this hidden epidemic.

Intersections Inc. has been in the business of identity theft protection for more than 16 years; before there even was an identity theft protection business. We help large banks help their customers and we are the engine behind IDENTITY GUARD®—a brand, which in my opinion stands apart in a field crowded with companies of questionable reputation. We invented the concept of data monitoring for consumers, and we continue to look for new ways that consumers can protect themselves and monitor their digital footprint— the birth of KID SURE^SM, our child identity theft product, being our latest innovation.

I remember when we first got the idea for KID SURE^SM. We knew child ID theft was a problem we wanted to solve right away. We wanted to be the first to market—and we weren't. We weren't because as with all of our endeavors, we won't put something on the market until we are absolutely sure it addresses the problems at-hand. And the products that were being released quickly were capitalizing on the hype and fear around child identity theft, but they weren't addressing the bigger problem—synthetic identity theft. We wanted to ensure our product, KID SURE^SM, would protect our customers from this kind of ID theft.

It took us over a year to build a product we were proud of. We could have released KID SURE^{SM} sooner, but it didn't meet our internal standards. The product actually has to work and provide value. KID SURE^{SM} does just that. It's the most comprehensive child ID theft product in the market. I don't mean to sound like a commercial, but I am very, very proud of what we've done.

But our quest is about far more than selling KID SURE^{SM}. We want to educate parents about child ID theft so that they can take matters in their own hands and do everything they can to keep their kids safe. This book is a great starting point.

I am proud to be associated with Intersections, IDENTITY GUARD® and The Children's Miracle Network, the beneficiary of the proceeds from this book. I know there was a lot of scary information in this book. I am a parent of two kids myself and I know how overwhelming the problem can be. But what I'm proud of, and why I stand behind this book, is that this is a book about educating parents.

Once you understand how serious this problem can get, I believe you will be better prepared to protect your kids. This is a case where knowledge really does equal power. This book is one of the tools you might choose to use, our product, KID SURE^{SM}, is another. And those are just two of dozens of ways you just might be able to reduce the risk of child ID theft happening to your kid, or at the very least, to catch it and recover from it as quickly as possible, with as little damage as possible.

Intersections's products are all about giving you the information and data you need to take your financial future into your own hands. With this book, and with our patent-pending KID SURE^{SM} product, we are taking that to the next level so parents can do what they do best—protect their kids.

So, as it turns out, Joe's "crazy" idea to write a book was actually pretty inspired. I am thankful his commitment has brought us to this point and I hope you walk away from this better prepared to protect what you treasure, in whatever way feels best to you.

Steve Schwartz
Chantilly, VA
July 2012

ABOUT THE AUTHOR

Virginia dad, Joe Mason, had had enough. After spending more than a decade helping adults protect themselves from identity theft and credit fraud, Joe thought he had heard and seen it all, until two years ago when he began to uncover the hidden nightmare over 140,000 American parents have faced—child identity theft.

A parent of two children himself, and the executive behind the acclaimed identity protection service, IDENTITY GUARD®, Joe was shocked to discover child identity theft had grown to epidemic proportions. He found that a prolonged weak economy, stricter immigration laws, and security vulnerabilities that come with increased online and mobile use were just some of the reasons for the alarming rise. What frustrated Joe even more was that neither the victims nor their parents discovered the crime until years later, when it was often too late for justice to be served.

Desperate to help these parents, Joe worked along-side Intersections' President of Partner Services, Steve Schwartz, to promote create KID SURE℠, the most comprehensive service of its kind for monitoring the Social Security numbers and personally identifiable information of children. But he isn't stopping there. Joe and his team at IDENTITY GUARD®, have set off on a mission to educate and empower parents around the country to stand up and fight back against organized crime, illegal immigrants, and even wayward family members who are kidnapping the identities of 16 innocent children each hour.

Joe Mason is a husband and father of two living in Haymarket, Virginia. He is the Senior Vice President of IDENTITYGUARD.com, a portal with solutions and information about identity theft protection that is owned and operated by Intersections Inc. Throughout his career, Joe has played a role in protecting the identities of well over three million Americans. Prior to joining Intersections, Joe spent nearly a decade at Capital One, where he managed their identity protection offerings and helped consumers understand the importance of protecting their personal information. Joe has a B.S. from the University of Virginia and an M.B.A. from The College of William and Mary and has been featured on CNN, Fox News, ABC News, and many other regional and national media outlets.

BANKRUPT AT BIRTH

ADDITIONAL RESOURCES

To accompany the book, we've included invaluable bonus materials so you can proactively protect your children against identity theft.

Throughout the book, you'll see Shield Icons that will point you where to go to collect your free resources. Here's what you'll get:

» The Quick Start Guide to Child ID Theft

» The Daily Shield Identity Theft eBook

» Risk Factors Checklist

» The Child ID Theft Safety Tele-class

» Video: Child ID Theft: A Growing Problem

» 10 Ways to Protect Your Smartphone, Laptop and Tablet

» Video: Emily's Story

» 30-Day trial of IDENTITY GUARD®†

 Visit **www.BankruptAtBirthBook.com** for additional resources.

RESOURCES

INTRODUCTION

1. 1. Javelin Strategy & Research, 2012 Identity Fraud Report: Social Media and Mobile Forming the New Fraud Frontier, Feb. 2012

CHAPTER ONE

2. ITRC Fact Sheet 110
3. http://redtape.msnbc.msn.com/_news/2011/07/07/7027882-america-down-but-not-out-a-nation-of-fighters-responds?lite
4. http://boston.cbslocal.com/tag/zach-friesen/
5. http://www.digtriad.com/news/local/article/229381/57/Reidsville-Man-Someone-Else-Claimed-My-Son-On-Their-Taxes
6. http://www.ftc.gov/bcp/workshops/stolenfutures/ - Transcript
7. Huffington Post 5/12/12 plus interviews on KHAS-TV and other media reports
8. Huffington Post story dated 8/22/11 plus ID theft 911 story and subsequent media stories

CHAPTER TWO

1. Stolen Futures Transcript plus subsequent media interviews and reports

CHAPTER THREE

1. http://chicago.cbslocal.com/2012/04/02/more-cases-of-elgin-id-theft-surface/
2. Des Moines Register May 17, 2012
3. http://newyork.cbslocal.com/2012/05/18/residents-of-teaneck-falling-

prey-to-outbreak-of-id-theft-credit-card-fraud/

4. http://thebatavian.com/howard-owens/grand-jury-report-man-accused-trying-injure-state-trooper-car/31104

5. Bulletin issued by the Elberton County Sherriff's Office (http://www.elbertcountysheriff.com)

6. http://www.theregister.co.uk/2005/03/21/brazil_phishing_arrest/

7. http://bangordailynews.com/2012/05/10/education/university-of-maine-server-hacked-data-may-have-been-stolen/

8. http://www.charlotteobserver.com/2012/05/14/3239381/security-breach-on-york-county.html

9. Data Breach Investigations Report (DBIR) (http://www.verizonbusiness.com/us/about/events/2012dbir/

10. 2012 ITRC Breach Report (http://www.idtheftcenter.org/ITRC%20Breach%20Report%202012.pdf)

11. http://www.usatoday.com/money/perfi/credit/2009-01-20-heartland-credit-card-security-breach_N.htm

12. http://www.wrdw.com/crimeteam12/headlines/Former_SC_DHHS_employee_arrested__148126225.html

13. http://www.tampabay.com/news/publicsafety/crime/49-accused-of-tax-fraud-and-identity-theft/1189406

14. http://www.tampagov.net/appl_tampa_announcements/ViewRelease.asp?ReleaseID=8414

15. http://articles.sun-sentinel.com/2012-06-09/news/fl-ftl-id-theft-tax-fraud-20120608_1_tax-returns-fraudulent-tax-million-tax-fraud

16. http://www.justice.gov/usao/flm/press/2012/june/20120606_Brown.html

17. http://www.suntimes.com/news/8613327-418/id-thieves-cash-in-on-dead-childrens-ss-numbers.html

18. Statement of Michael J. Astrue before the House Committee on Ways and Means, Subcommittee on Social Security February 2, 2012

19. http://abcnews.go.com/GMA/medical-identity-theft-protect-identity/story?id=10047398

20. http://www.asrn.org/journal-nursing-today/627-id-thieves-target-admitted-patients-medical-records.html

CHAPTER FOUR

1. http://heraldnews.suntimes.com/news/crime/12468809-418/boling-

brook-woman-accused-of-stealing-aunts-identity.html
2. http://www.idtheftconsumerinfo.com/2012/05/id-theft-by-sisters-devastates-woman/
3. Javelin Strategy & Research, 2012 Identity Fraud Report: Social Media and Mobile Forming the New Fraud Frontier, Feb. 2012
4. http://articles.herald-mail.com/2011-12-16/news/30527318_1_grubb-landing-rebecca-jean-ferguson-identity
5. http://www.justice.gov/usao/nj/Press/files/Ko,%20Jung-Sook%20Sentencing%20News%20Release.html
6. http://www.ice.gov/news/releases/1203/120316lasvegas.htm
7. http://www.wyff4.com/GHS-Fires-Employee-Facing-Identity-Theft-Charges/-/9324882/10075454/-/ogimjmz/-/index.html
8. http://waysandmeans.house.gov/UploadedFiles/Lanius_Testimony.pdf
9. http://judiciary.house.gov/hearings/printers/112th/112-105_73860.PDF
10. http://www.oregonlive.com/portland/index.ssf/2011/01/john_doe_who_stole_murdered_bo.html

CHAPTER FIVE

1. OIG, Kindergarten through 12th Grade Schools' Collection and Use of Social Security Numbers, July 2010. (http://oig.ssa.gov/kindergarten-through-12th-grade-schools-collection-and-use-social-security-numbers)
2. http://safeschoolsapp.com/2011/09/06/2-birdville-students-hack-into-school-district%E2%80%99s-network/
3. http://www.washingtonpost.com/wp-dyn/content/article/2010/01/28/AR2010012803494.html
4. CNN, April 1, 2009 (http://topics.cnn.com/topics/identity_theft)
5. http://www.secure128.com/el-paso-school-district-breach-highlights-need-for-data-security.aspx
6. Raleigh News Observer, December 5, 2009 (http://www.newsobserver.com/2009/12/05/226344/kids-social-security-numbers-on.html)
7. SSA Inspector General's Report (http://oig.ssa.gov/report-fraud-waste-or-abuse/what-cant-oig-investigate/identity-theft)
8. Knoxville News Sentinel April 9, 2009 (http://www.knoxnews.com/

news/2009/apr/09/18000-nashville-students-personal-data-put-on-line/)

9. Bay News 9, May 10, 2012 (http://www.baynews9.com/content/news/articles/bn9/2012/5/10/students_information.html)

10. Inspector's General's Report, Miami-Dade County Public Schools, 2/2/2012

11. US Attorney Southern District of Florida, Press Release August 19, 2009

12. WALB Report March 19, 2012 (http://www.walb.com/story/17150499/teen-charged-with-multiple-counts-of-identity-theft)

13. BBC, June 30, 2010 (http://www.bbc.co.uk/news/10444151)

14. DOJ Fact Sheet

CHAPTER SIX

1. Facebook 8K filing June 25, 2012

2. CNET June 2, 2012, White Paper: "Power of Like2".

3. "Why Facebook Users Get more than they Give" 2/3/12 (http://pewInternet.org/Reports/2012/Facebook-users/Summary/About.aspx)

4. Media Bistro, February 21, 2012 (http://www.mediabistro.com/alltwitter/500-million-registered-users_b18842)

5. U.S. Teen Mobile Report:"Calling Yesterday, Texting Today, Using Apps Tomorrow," October 14, 2010

6. Tech Crunch, March 14, 2012 (http://techcrunch.com/2012/03/14/this-is-everything-you-need-to-know-about-pinterest-infographic/)

7. Tech Crunch, April 13, 2012 (http://techcrunch.com/2012/04/13/instagrams-user-count-now-at-40-million-saw-10-million-new-users-in-last-10-days/)

8. Entertainment Software Association, Industry Facts (http://www.theesa.com/facts/index.asp)

9. Cylabs, Child Identity Theft Study(www.cylab.cmu.edu/files/pdfs/reports/2011/child-identity-theft.pdf)

10. Rotenberg testimony, April 29, 2010 (http://epic.org/privacy/kids/EPIC_COPPA_Testimony_042910.pdf)

11. Senate Committee on the Judiciary Subcommittee on Privacy, Technology, and the Law, Jan 31, 2012.

12. FTC Paper: "Talking About ID Theft."

13. COPPA (http://www.ftc.gov/privacy/privacyinitiatives/childrens.html)

14. WSGR Alert: September 2011 FTC Proposes Significant Revisions To Children's Online Privacy Protection Rule
15. COPPA (http://www.ftc.gov/os/1999/06/kidsprivacy.htm)
16. Europe vs. Facebook (http://europe-v-facebook.org/EN/Data_Pool/data_pool.html)
17. Huffington Post, July 22-23, 2011 (http://www.huffington-post.com/2011/07/22/george-bronk-sentenced-facebook-stalking_n_907506.html/)
18. http://www.minormonitor.com/infographic/kids-on-facebook/
19. CR 5/10/2011 (http://www.consumerreports.org/cro/magazine-archive/2011/june/electronics-computers/state-of-the-net/facebook-concerns/index.htm)
20. "Why parents help their children lie about their age to Facebook: http://firstmonday.org/htbin/cgiwrap/bin/ojs/index.php/fm/article/view/3850/3075
21. MSN Now, May 28, 2012
22. Morrison & Foerster Client Alert. COPPA Changes Proposed, September 21, 2011

CHAPTER SEVEN

1. NYT Aug. 11, 2010 (http://www.nytimes.com/2010/08/12/technology/personaltech/12basics.html)
2. WWLP News Report May 1, 2012 (http://www.wwlp.com/dpp/news/i_team/facebook-birthdays-and-identity-theft)
3. "Online game sites can be cute, pink, and infected", Jan 12, 2012 http://www.avast.com/en-us/pr-avast-software-online-game-sites-can-be-cute-pink-and-infected
4. FTC Release 03/27/2012. (http://ftc.gov/opa/2012/03/rockyou.shtm)

CHAPTER EIGHT

1. "Teens and Sexting", Pew Foundation, December 15, 2009,
2. http://www.dosomething.org/blog/chatterbox/florida-teen-busted-sexting
3. SB 242 (http://info.sen.ca.gov/pub/11-12/bill/sen/sb_0201-0250/

sb_242_bill_20110502_amended_sen_v98.html)

CHAPTER NINE

1. Dallas News, April 11, 2011 (http://www.dallasnews.com/news/state/headlines/20110411-breach-in-texas-comptrollers-office-exposes-3.5-million-social-security-numbers-birth-dates.ece)
2. Stolen Futures transcript
3. Maryland HB 555(http://mlis.state.md.us/2012rs/billfile/hb0555.htm)
4. Zucker Press Release, Jan. 12, 2012 (http://www.craigzucker.com/)
5. http://www.oregonlive.com/happy-valley/index.ssf/2012/04/identity_theft_sends_innocent.html
6. Nov. 13, 2009 (http://www.katu.com/news/69946642.html)

CHAPTER TEN

1. Dallas News, February 19, 2012 & March 19, 2012